RELIGION IN THE SOUTH

Religion in the South

Essays by
JOHN B. BOLES
C. ERIC LINCOLN
DAVID EDWIN HARRELL, JR.
J. WAYNE FLYNT
SAMUEL S. HILL
EDWIN S. GAUSTAD

Edited by
CHARLES REAGAN WILSON

UNIVERSITY PRESS OF MISSISSIPPI
Jackson

THIS BOOK HAS BEEN SPONSORED BY
THE UNIVERSITY OF MISSISSIPPI

Library of Congress Cataloging in Publication Data
Main entry under title:

Religion in the South.

(Chancellor's symposium series ; 1984)
Papers presented at the Porter L. Fortune Chancellor's
Symposium on Southern History at the University of
Mississippi, 3–5 October 1984, sponsored by the University
of Mississippi.
Bibliography: p.
Includes index.
1. Southern States—Religion—Congresses. I. Boles,
John B. II. Wilson, Charles Reagan. III. University of
Mississippi. IV. Porter L. Fortune Chancellor's Symposium
on Southern History (1984 : University of Mississippi)
V. Series.
BR535.R437   1985   200'.975   85-5361
ISBN 0-87805-256-9
ISBN 0-87805-257-7 (pbk.)

Contents

Preface

These essays were originally prepared for the Porter L. Fortune Chancellor's Symposium on Southern History at the University of Mississippi. On October 3–5, 1984, scholars from across the nation gathered on the campus at Oxford, Mississippi, to consider the topic "Religion in the South."

Religion is an abiding human concern. Societies throughout history have grappled in different ways with trying to understand the spiritual dimension of life. Religion and culture have been close in the South, so one has the chance to observe how religious values and institutions both shape and reflect a society's overall outlook. Evangelical Protestantism has been the South's dominant tradition. Although it has been a vital part of American religious history, evangelical Protestantism has never achieved in any other society the influence it has had in the South. What has this religious tradition offered to the southern people, black and white, what role has it played in their history, that has enabled it to endure? How has it affected people living in the region who are not part of the dominant tradition? The symposium participants addressed themselves to these broad human concerns, and this volume contains their reflections.

Planning and implementing the symposium was a cooperative effort. The Mississippi Committee for the Humanities and the National Endowment for the Humanities generously funded the conference, and thanks are due the staffs of both organizations, especially Dr. Cora Norman of the Mississippi Committee.

Commentators at the conference included Kenneth K. Bailey, Randall M. Miller, Jean E. Friedman, James M. Washington, Edward Akin, and Leslie B. McLemore. They performed their task well, and their commentaries stimulated further discussion. Joseph L. Howze, Mary John Dye, Thea Bowman, Sylvester

Oliver, Twick Morrison, and Polly Williams served as moderators of the sessions.

My colleagues in the Department of History and the Center for the Study of Southern Culture offered essential advice and encouragement. I relied on them at every stage and appreciate their genuine support. Fred Laurenzo played a particularly important role in assuming responsibility for many of the logistical details during the symposium. Graduate students from the Department of History, members of Phi Alpha Theta, and the staffs of the Department of History and the Center for the Study of Southern Culture worked quietly behind the scenes to make the conference a success. Ann Summer Holmes, Rebecca Bowers, Martha Doyel, Karen McDearman, Debra Northart, and Sarah Dixon offered crucial assistance.

RELIGION IN THE SOUTH

Introduction

CHARLES REAGAN WILSON

Religion has been a powerful force in creating and maintaining southern regional distinctiveness. Beginning with the frontier revivals of the early nineteenth century, evangelical Protestantism became the dominant religious impulse of the South. In the antebellum period the region's churches were the first institutions to divide from the North over the slavery issue, and the Baptists, Methodists, and Presbyterians maintained sectionally organized, institutionally powerful denominations long after the Civil War. Studies of southern religious attitudes and behavior by sociologists and others show that the Protestant churches remain crucial to understanding the region today.

Southern religion has gained a new public prominence through certain movements within the recent evangelical resurgence. Groups like the Moral Majority, based in Virginia, have become an influential part of the New Right movement, although neither Moral Majority nor the New Right is predominantly southern. The electronic church, which is dominated by evangelists such as Pat Robertson in Virginia, Jim Bakker in North Carolina, and Jimmy Swaggart in Louisiana, is now combining modern technology and financing with its message of the "Old Time Religion." A born-again southerner was elected president in 1976 and his successor gained southern evangelical votes in 1980 and 1984, with religion prominently discussed in both campaigns. Adding another dimension in 1984 was the emergence of a southern born-and-raised black minister as a major presidential candidate, utilizing southern black churches as a primary base of support.

In spite of a general recognition of its importance, less is known about southern religious life than about political, military,

3

economic, and literary topics. Even as recently as the early
1960s, most books on southern religion were uncritical institutional histories of denominations or admiring biographies of
ministers. Beginning in the mid-1960s scholars from many disciplines and perspectives have increasingly studied the historical
development and contemporary significance of religion in the
South. John B. Boles surveyed the field in a 1982 historiographical essay and concluded that "southern religion has become a
tradition recovered." The publication of Samuel S. Hill's *Encyclopedia of Religion in the South* in late 1984 symbolized the
coming of age of the field of southern religious studies. The
appearance of Charles H. Lippy's *Bibliography of Religion in the
South* in 1985 will reinforce its new standing.[1]

Research on southern religion has focused on understanding
the character and distinctiveness of the evangelical Protestant
tradition. Kenneth K. Bailey's *Southern White Protestantism in
the Twentieth Century* (1964) was the first modern study to
achieve an interdenominational perspective on southern religion
and to place it in a national context. Working in an earlier time
period, John B. Boles, in *The Great Revival, 1787–1805: The
Origins of the Southern Evangelical Mind* (1972) and *Religion in
Antebellum Kentucky* (1976), traced the emergence of a southern
evangelical consensus in the early nineteenth century, especially
the popular-folk worldview in the region. Donald G. Mathews's
Religion in the Old South (1977) was a sweeping, provocative
overview of the evangelical impact in the antebellum period,
including the role of women and blacks in the churches.

The dominant force in the study of religion in the South has
been Samuel S. Hill. His *Southern Churches in Crisis,* published
in 1964 during the height of the region's racial conflict, was a
unique study of the historical and theological background of contemporary southern Protestantism. In this and other works Hill
has posited and analyzed an interdenominational southern
evangelical tradition, arguing for its distinctive structure, ritual,
theology, and style. Drawing upon history, sociology, political

science, theology, and other disciplines, Hill has been receptive
to new methodologies and approaches to the study of southern
religion.

Indeed, perhaps the most significant development in recent
studies of southern religion has been the appearance of works
with sophisticated conceptualization, drawing on disciplines
other than history. Thomas Virgil Peterson's *Ham and Japheth:
The Mythic World of Whites in the Antebellum South* (1978), the
work of a scholar trained in religious studies, used the anthropological concepts of Clifford Geertz and Claude Leví-
Strauss in analyzing the racial mythology of the South. Charles
Reagan Wilson's *Baptized in Blood: The Religion of the Lost
Cause, 1865–1920* (1980) employed anthropological and sociological models in arguing for the existence of a southern civil religion
after the Civil War. The most sophisticated study of southern
religion is Rhys Isaac's *The Transformation of Virginia, 1740–
1790* (1982). Isaac, a historian, utilizes insights from the field of
symbolic anthropology in identifying the "cognitive structures,"
the cultural models and worldviews, of eighteenth-century Virginia and, more broadly, the South.

The present volume offers the reader a convenient overview of
southern religious development, through studies of key aspects
of that history. It concentrates on the dominant evangelical tradition. A volume this size cannot claim to be exhaustive. Its approach is to focus on crucial time periods—the antebellum years,
the late nineteenth century, and the contemporary era. The concern is to examine topics that are central to understanding southern religion—the origins of the evangelical consensus and of
black religion, the nature of religious diversity in the South, the
extent of a Social Gospel impulse, the distinctiveness of the region's outlook on religious–political activities, and the dimensions of the South's "culture religion" in comparison with others
in the nation. Additional topics need to be explored, of course,
and the hope is to stimulate further research.

In the first essay John B. Boles examines the origins of the

evangelical tradition in the Old South. Boles questions the conventional wisdom of the importance of the First Great Awakening
in the late colonial South, concluding that it "has in general been
exaggerated, especially in length and geographical scope." Boles
discusses the prerequisite conditions for religious revivals occurring, and he argues that these conditions were not met in the
South as a whole until the 1790s. Religious people saw that decade as a time of "catastrophic religious decline," and the result of
that perception was the Great Revival of 1800–05—the turning
point in southern religious history. The intense revivalism at the
camp meetings in Logan County, Kentucky, led to an enduring
religious worldview and forms of worship that would lead to the
evangelical dominance of the South. "To a remarkable degree,"
Boles writes, "evangelical religion shaped the mentalité of antebellum southerners, rich and poor, slaveholder and nonslaveholder." Boles chronicles the remarkable transformation of
evangelical sects from a position of dissenting outcasts in society
into accommodation to, and acceptance by, that society. Most
notably, the same religious sects that had once opposed the
slaveholding aristocracy came to defend southern society, including slavery, in order to win cultural approval, or at least tolera-
tion, for the spread of their religious message. Boles also,
though, stresses the existence of "a biracial religious culture in
the antebellum South." In religious institutions "slaves were
treated more nearly as equals than anywhere else in the society."
Finally, Boles points out that religion made white democracy
possible in the Old South by reducing class tensions and that the
churches provided an institutional focus for the personal development of white women in the region.

    Recent books by Clarence E. Walker and Hans A. Baer have
explored institutional and cultural aspects of black religion after
the Civil War, but the study of Afro-American religion in the
South generally has focused on the antebellum period. In the
1970s historians of slavery such as Eugene Genovese, George

Rawick, and John W. Blassingame made religion a central part of
their studies of the peculiar institution. Lawrence W. Levine
analyzed black folklife and portrayed the importance of religion
to the slave worldview, and Albert J. Raboteau published a
definitive study of the "invisible institution" of slave religion.[2]
Historians like Donald G. Mathews, John B. Boles, and Kenneth K. Bailey have outlined white Protestantism's delayed but
important missionary efforts to the slaves in the early nineteenth
century.

C. Eric Lincoln's paper is a thorough summary of black religious history from the settlement of Jamestown to the coming of
the Civil War. He shows the slowness with which American
Christians acted in sharing their spiritual message with blacks,
but he concludes that "Christianity did eventually establish deep
roots in the black subculture, and there it became the organizing
matrix of the black experience." Lincoln discusses the role of
blacks in camp meetings, and he catalogues a list of black
preachers, some of whom had followings among whites as well as
blacks. In this wide-ranging overview, Lincoln covers the emergence of separate black denominations, the dimensions of the
"invisible church" (the underground church operating indepen-
dently of white control in the slave quarters), the efforts of white
slaveholders to use the Christian message for control of the
slaves, and the nature of black worship, whether in the context of
biracial worship or in the separate black church. Lincoln and
Boles disagree in regard to the extent of black-white religious
interaction in the Old South. Lincoln grants that "the prevailing
custom was for white and black Christians to worship in the same
white church, usually attending the same services," but he argues that the more important points were blacks were not allowed an equal role in church deliberations and they were fed a
gospel distorted to teach them obedience. A recent article by
Kenneth K. Bailey seems to support the view that, in Boles's
words, "the normative worship experience of slaves was in a

biracial church, where—despite clear inequalities and white prejudice—blacks heard the full gospel preached and achieved a significant degree of spiritual freedom."

David Edwin Harrell, Jr., had a seemingly impossible assignment in relating the experiences of Roman Catholics, Jews, and Protestant sectarians in living under the South's evangelical hegemony. Few interpretive monographs exist on the history of these groups, although recent edited volumes represent promising beginnings of research.[3] Eli Evans's *The Provincials: A Personal History of Jews in the South* (1976) is a particularly engaging combination of history and memoir.

Harrell, the leading student of sectarianism in the South, in a witty and provocative essay brings the three groups together under the rubric, "religious pluralism." Acknowledging that "anti-Catholicism and anti-Semitism ebbed and flowed in southern history," he points out that, on the other hand, for the most part Catholics and Jews "felt perfectly at home with their southern religious neighbors." Catholics, Jews, and sectarians in the South have participated in, and helped to shape, the major aspects of southern life. He argues that the best approach to understanding religious diversity in the South is "to inject class tension into the study of southern religion." Harrell analyzes the development of religious class tension from the early nineteenth century, with the emergence of the Baptists and the Methodists as classic sectarians, through the blurring of class tensions in the Civil War, to the sectarian turmoil at the turn of the twentieth century. Harrell shows the tensions within denominations, as well as the appearance of new religious groups such as the Pentecostals, the Holiness movement, and the Churches of Christ. His conclusion is that "the 1890s were a watershed in southern religious history as well as in southern political history." This interpretation offers rich possibilities for futher relating developments in religious history to the broader cultural context of the South.

Southern religion has usually been portrayed as otherworldly and uninterested in society. Recent scholarship suggests, however, that southern churches have been concerned with society, not with social reform but with maintaining moral values and evangelical dominance. Historians once argued that the Social Gospel movement of the early twentieth century did not exist in the South at all, but most now acknowledge its existence, although a historiographical debate remains over the extent of its influence.[4] A recent book by John Patrick McDowell outlines the social ministries of women within the Methodist Episcopal Church, South, which was the denomination that showed the greatest commitment to progressive social concerns. Most southern historians would probably still maintain, however, that the Social Gospel was a minor theme in most southern religious groups and that it expressed itself more in terms of ameliorative charity than in attempts to change social structures.

J. Wayne Flynt offers a vigorous advocacy for the existence of a Social Gospel tradition in the South, focusing on a case study of the Presbyterian Church in the United States in the first two decades of the twentieth century. The southern Presbyterians were conservative theologically and socially and seem the least likely to have Social Gospel concerns. Flynt's paper nonetheless shows reform-minded activists such as Edwin O. Guerrant, A. W. McAllister, Hallie Winsborough, Alexander McKelway, and, above all, Walter Lingle, an overlooked but intriguing figure in southern religious history. A discussion of Lingle's experiences in promoting social concern anchors the article, which also discusses the Presbyterian social welfare efforts in Appalachia, in cities, and in the Country Life Movement. Flynt portrays the opposition to such efforts within the church, admits the denomination's failure to address fully race-related problems, and argues for the significant role of women in the southern version of a Social Gospel, the latter a theme long stressed by Anne Firor Scott. Flynt insists that the Social Gospel simply had a different look in the South than in the North, where urban problems at that period of time were of pressing importance. "Obviously a

region with few cities would produce religious concerns somewhat different from a region with many cities," he writes. When
the Social Gospel was interjected into "rural America it assumed
new directions." The debate on the extent of the Social Gospel's
penetration in the region's local churches will continue, but
Flynt has offered striking institutional and individual evidence
for his viewpoint.

Flynt's article shows, then, that southern religion has not been
as myopically otherworldly as the stereotype of it would suggest,
a conclusion further reinforced by examining the relationship
between religion and politics in the South. Historically, southern
churches have mobilized to use politics to achieve moral ends—
most notably in the moral reform efforts for blue laws, the restriction of gambling, and especially the prohibition of the sale of
alcoholic beverages. The contributors to a recent collection of
essays on religious-political interaction in the South stressed that
the fundamentalist influence in the recent South has been the
key factor in making southern religious-political activities different from those elsewhere. Further, southern religion has made
its greatest contemporary political impact in regard to moral and
social issues.[5]

In his essay, Samuel S. Hill puts this recent religious–political
interaction into historical and typological perspective. Using in-
terdisciplinary methods, he outlines four kinds of religious–
political enterprises in the South. He argues that the normative
southern position on religion and politics is unique, deriving
from the theology and methods of revivalistic Protestantism,
from a Calvinistic belief that church and state should cooperate in
building a holy society, and from a faith that individuals should
embody righteous behavior in daily life. This outlook is not
classic conservatism. "Southern political concern," Hill writes,
"has not sought to lessen the role of government, rather to place
the right quality of people in office." With that background, Hill
analyzes the 1976 and 1980 presidential elections and the 1984
North Carolina senatorial campaign, in which incumbent Senator

Jesse Helms was narrowly reelected. He concludes that the moral agenda of the New Christian Right reflects some traditional concerns of church people in the region but in other ways "it sounds a little different from what they are accustomed to hearing."

The emergence of southern religious history as a distinct field includes its increasing incorporation into the broader field of American religious studies. In a 1964 historiographical essay on American religious history, Henry F. May discussed no studies of southern religion among the significant works of the previous thirty years.[6] In 1972, however, Sydney E. Ahlstrom's *A Religious History of the American People* did include chapters on southern developments, and surveys of American religion since then typically have included at least references to the region.[7] Cultural geographers such as James R. Shortridge and Roger W. Stump and religious demographers such as Edwin S. Gaustad have also begun exploring the geographical dimensions of American religion, mapping the South's distinctiveness as a cultural area in the nation and the diversity existing in the region's subcultures.[8]

As Gaustad points out in his essay, the regional character of American religion in general represents a major source of its diversity. He carefully outlines the history and current state of regionalism in religion, with special attention to the South's patterns in comparison to the wider context of national trends. The South's first religious establishment was not evangelical but the Church of England, which enjoyed official recognition and dominance in the southern colonies. The Quakers and the Baptists secured influence in the Carolinas, though, and the Anglicans failed to penetrate interior areas. In the nineteenth century the Methodists and the Baptists conquered the frontier and, in the process, the South as well. Gaustad discusses a wide array of religious groups that have dominated particular regions of the nation, and he identifies four "culture religions" today—"the Lutheran in the upper Midwest, the Baptist in the Southeast, the

Mormon in the far West, and the Roman Catholic in the North-east and Southwest." Despite the supposed homogenizing factors in modern American life, Gaustad concludes that "the homogenization has still a very long way to go in religion." Looking more closely at the South itself, Gaustad suggests the religious diversity within the region, including the geographical distribution of Roman Catholicism, the Churches of Christ, the Cumberland Presbyterians, and the Pentecostals. Gaustad's paper is valuable in showing the extent and the limitations of the evangelical hegemony in the South.

Despite other changes in the South, southerners today continue to hold to certain patterns in religious matters. Sociologist John Shelton Reed has analyzed survey data that shows southerners go to church more often than those in other regions, watch religious broadcasts more frequently, give more money to churches, and are more likely to believe in a literal devil and a heaven and a hell. Religion continues to influence such cultural expressions as country, blues, and gospel music and literature. The South's "religious culture" does not have the grip on the region that it once did, but it remains central to the idea of southern distinctiveness.

Through much of their history, the southern people have lived a hard life, and religion was especially important to them in sustaining themselves. C. Vann Woodward has argued that the region's historical experiences created a tragic view of life.[9] This outlook nurtured a particular kind of religious tradition, and these essays explore the relationship between historical experience and religious expression.

Evangelical Protestantism in the Old South:
From Religious Dissent to Cultural Dominance

JOHN B. BOLES

A symposium such as this one, on religion in the South, would have been almost inconceivable only twenty years ago. Scholarly study of the history of southern religion is that new. Of course there are exceptions to all generalizations, and one should hasten to mention the pioneering scholarship of such students as Walter B. Posey, Wesley M. Gewehr, and Hunter D. Farish. Yet most work on religion in the South was of the filiopietistic sort, stories of heroes of the church, or one-sided denominational histories that cast the favored denomination in an unfailingly flattering light. When Henry F. May in an important historiographical essay in the 1964 *American Historical Review* praised the "recovery" of American religious history, he did not mention a single title on southern religion.[1] But what a difference two decades makes! In 1964 Kenneth K. Bailey published his *Southern White Protestantism in the Twentieth Century*, two years later Samuel S. Hill, Jr., followed with *Southern Churches in Crisis*, and the modern field of southern religious history was launched. Dozens of important books, scores of dissertations and articles, an encyclopedia, and several symposia later, we can now assess the role of religion in the South, an assessment made possible by the discovery of southern religious history during the last twenty years. Today it would take an extremely bold—or foolish— historian to write about the "course of the South to secession"

13

without taking religion into account. Now evangelical Protestantism is understood to have been an essential ingredient of antebellum southern culture, and thanks to the recent scholarship historians have a better idea of how "the religious mind of the Old South" evolved. That development, and its consequences, are the topic here.

The whites who settled the Chesapeake, the Carolinas, and later Georgia brought with their cluster of British cultural values vaguely held Protestant beliefs, but the weakness of the institutional church—even after Anglicanism was officially established—compounded by the inadequacies of many of the clergy and the dispersed pattern of settlement, made a strong religious life almost impossible. Beginning in the 1740s evangelical denominations began to penetrate the southern colonies, but there was to be no transformation of the South as a whole until the first few decades of the nineteenth century. The First Great Awakening of textbook fame did not really occur in the South in the mid-eighteenth century as it did in New England and certain Middle Atlantic regions. In fact, the South's first "great awakening" did not come until 1800–1805 in a period of religious excitement often called the "Great Revival."

Explaining nonevents is always difficult, especially when all the weight of textbook authority suggests otherwise. The First Great Awakening has in general been exaggerated, especially in length and geographical scope.[2] Rather than stretching from the 1720s to roughly the 1790s, and sweeping up and down the thirteen colonies tieing them together in some proto-nationalistic sense, the Great Awakening—if "great" implies a high level of religious intensity and near universal appeal at least in specific locales—should be confined to the early 1740s only, and geographically to specific regions in Massachusetts, Connecticut, Pennsylvania, and New Jersey. Even in those years and in those regions, the label "Great Awakening" seems to have been applied only retrospectively by later historians. Because of the historiographical paradigm of a Great Awakening in the middle decades of the eighteenth century, however, the occurrence of a revival here and there in the South has been assumed to prove there was a southern Great Awakening. This of course is tautological reasoning, and since there has not been a single year in which at least one outbreak of revivalism has not occurred, it allows those who favor an expansive definition of the Great Awakening to stretch the concept to cover most of America during most of the eighteenth century. That ballooned interpretation needs to be punctured. If one carefully examines the accounts of revivalism in the Carolinas and Georgia in the 1740s through 1790s, or follows George Whitefield in his travels across the South, or studies the three "phases" of the so-called Virginia Great Awakening, one does in fact find many accounts of localized revivals, or repeated mini-awakenings, but never is a general region caught up in the sort of intense, practically universal (at least temporarily) religious frenzy that the term *Great* Awakening suggests.[3] Why not? Why was not the South, the eventual Bible Belt, swept up in the religious movement that set parts of New England aflame?

Before a powerful religious revival can occur, several prerequisite conditions have to be met. There must be in place a network of churches and ministers, there must be a shared community of belief about how God works in history, and there must be a shared sense of religious and social-cultural crisis so intense that many believe only divine intervention can set things aright. Those prerequisites existed in wide portions of New England and the Middle Atlantic colonies in the 1730s, but they were noticeably absent in the southern colonies. Not until the very end of the 1790s were they met in the South as a whole, and then a resounding series of revivals erupted like a religious epidemic: the Great Revival. What happened in the 1740s through 1770s, most clearly in Virginia, was the gradual achievement of the prerequisites for a general awakening. The revivals in Virginia before the Revolution did not transform the colony, but they provided the foundation for the later series of revivals and protracted meetings that did fundamentally alter the religious center of gravity.

In his classic study five decades ago Wesley M. Gewehr described what he called the Great Awakening in Virginia as having three distinct phases—a Presbyterian revival beginning in the early 1740s, a Baptist revival beginning about 1760, and a Methodist revival beginning about 1770. The first two revivals declined after about ten years and the Methodist phase was cut short by the Revolution. This categorization of the Virginia revivals into three separate movements, occurring in different portions of the colony and each confined to one denomination, is still valid and in part suggests why the three unrelated movements did not either separately or together constitute a true "Great" Awakening. This is not the place to rehearse the details of these Virginia events. It is important, however, to recognize the combined results. Each denominational phase produced a number of churches, a corps of committed ministers, and small, localized religious communities of persons who shared an evangelical world view.

The Presbyterians with their strong tradition of a learned ministry were not well-prepared to cope with expansion in the southern backcountry, but the Baptists and Methodists seemed ideally suited for the kind of accommodation to frontier or semi-frontier realities that had stymied the Anglican church. The Baptists rejected the idea of a salaried, formally trained ministry, and their farmer-preachers, earning their own keep by weekday labor and speaking the vernacular, proved to be highly effective. The Methodists adopted an innovative organizational scheme, the itinerant system, whereby hardy ministers, mounted on horseback, stayed not at one church but instead traveled a broad circuit through the countryside, preaching on a regular schedule at specified locations—a cabin, a barn, a cooperating Anglican church, any public hall. Hence one Methodist itinerant could preach to far more persons than a settled minister and to smaller groups than would have been able to support their own full-time minister. A local "band" or "class" of laypersons took seriously the responsibility of supervising the group's morality and spiritual growth in the absence of the preacher. The Baptists utilized their monthly business meetings to oversee the group's behavior. Individuals were "cited" for conduct unbecoming to a Christian, and those so charged either repented or, after a "trial," if found guilty were excommunicated. This procedure was less an inquisition than a way for the group to work out for itself its own understanding of the nature of Christian life. There were examples of rigidity and harshness, of course, but also many examples of common people struggling with the problems of living a moral life under demanding conditions. Through such methods—and the Presbyterian presbyteries operated in roughly similar fashion—the evangelical life-style and the belief system within which it operated were standardized and legitimized across the South in the years just before and after the American Revolution. Hence two prerequisites for a general awakening—a network of churches and ministers, and a prevalent belief system—were in place by the mid-1780s in Virginia, and shortly thereafter in much of the seaboard South.[4]

The interdenominational revival that occurred in central Virginia for several years after 1785 indicated that the ingredients were present for a more general revival than the South had yet experienced. Baptists, Methodists, and Presbyterians, simultaneously and in contiguous regions, for the first time enjoyed a brief period of excitement and growth, and although the season soon ebbed, it had a significant impact on southern religion. First, it expanded still further the number of evangelical churches and increased substantially the total of active ministers. Second and as a result of the first, the constellation of beliefs and attitudes associated with evangelical religion became even more widespread. The acceptance of such beliefs, however, does not automatically translate into vigorous church membership, for persons can accept in a vague intellectual sense a system of values without reshaping their lives into conformity with those values. The presence of those values, however passive they might be, means that if a situation occurs that makes them more salient, persons might effect a shift in behavior. Events can be perceived in such a way that background beliefs, almost unconscious cultural attitudes, can be "activated" and come to the foreground. Religious revivals do not occur in a vacuum; rather they represent a response within a religious context to a felt sense of crisis. The Virginia revival of the mid-1780s seemed to promise a new age for the church in the Old Dominion, but soon that hope was dashed as the state fell into what was widely interpreted to be a religious decline. That sense of decline was exacerbated because it came in the aftermath of such promising times, and the perception of falling away contributed to a perception of crisis that soon gripped the South. The decade of the 1790s came to be seen as a period of catastrophic religious decline, and the reactions to that critical state proved to be the origins of the so-called Great Revival of 1800–1805.

There are several ways of explaining why the mid-1780s Virginia revival lasted only two or three years and failed to spread across the South. One plausible explanation points toward the volatile politics of the era. In the aftermath of the Revolution the Articles of Confederation government proved inadequate to the exigencies of the moment, and political controversy, intermingled with the declining economic fortunes of the young nation, combined to drive religious concerns from a prominent position in the minds of most people. Not only was one form of government being rejected and a new one being proposed and then fought through to ratification, but state-level politics were in flux also. Moreover, with the war over and the West open, farmers on the relatively worn-out soils of the Tidewater and Piedmont cast envious eyes toward the acclaimed lands over the Appalachians. It seemed to some observers that every tongue was awag about the opportunities to be found to the west, and the trails and wagon roads westward were soon crowded with ambitious pioneers. The fertility of the land and the anticipated profits crowded religious sentiments out of the imagination. Westward migration left small churches almost decimated in the eastern portion of Virginia and the seaboard South, and the newcomers in the West hardly had time for religion in the busy first years of carving out farmsteads, fighting Indians, taming the frontier. In piedmont South Carolina and Georgia the middle years of the 1790s saw a frenzy of activity as cotton cultivation exploded westward following the perfection of the cotton gin. These were hardly the years for religious expansion.

The Virginia mini awakening of the mid-1780s was localized, but an unusual number of ministers found their calling in its midst. Even before the revival waned, many of these ministers began moving west and southwest with their lay contemporaries. Occasional ministers in the Carolinas also moved westward as many of their flock sought fresh opportunities. These migrating ministers not only brought the seeds of faith from which western churches would eventually sprout, but they brought the memory of the temporary religious excitement of the mid-1780s (and earlier) and the desire to recapture in the loneliness of the West the sense of community associated with the former churches east of the Appalachians. The network of churches and ministers, and the religious belief system, were slowly spreading across the South in the decade of the 1790s while economic and political events—on the surface at least—seemed to be diminishing the religious prospects for the region. The infrastructure for potential religious growth was being established even as religious interest apparently was declining.[5]

Contemporaries, especially those who cared about the fortunes of Christianity, were much more aware of the troubling decline of religion than they were aware of the less obvious countervailing forces at work. Faced with half empty churches in the East and not yet built churches in the West, with political and economic speculation rampant everywhere, and then increasingly after the mid-1790s with the fear of French-style deism added to the more prosaic homegrown indifference, the faithful remnant began to despair. The hopes engendered by the mid-1780 revival were crushed, and some began to worry about even the survival of religion. Despair fed despair, and pessimism about the future became the dominant religious theme. In fact, absolute church membership in certain locales did drop, as did Methodist figures for the region as a whole. Ministerial morale plummeted as preachers corresponded and commiserated with one another. The so-called declension came to preoccupy most ministers and many laypersons; private correspondence, diaries, sermons, associational minutes, and pastoral letters testify to the deep concern with the state of religion. Had the American Revolution been won and a foretaste of revival been experienced only for the nation to founder in a malaise of religious depression?

Religion, as Clifford Geertz has reminded us, is a model of and for reality; it explains the perceived world and prescribes the right behavior.[6] Faced with spiritual decline, almost overwhelmed at times with hopelessness, clergy began in the early to mid-1790s to seek an explanation for the situation as they understood it. Central to their attempt to make sense of the apparent declension was their assumption that God was both omnipotent and omniscient. Hence God was aware of the dilemma, and because it was axiomatic that God was neither inefficient nor whimsical, the religious depression must somehow be part of His plan for mankind. But why would He allow—even send—a decline in religious vitality? Could he be seeking to teach erring mankind a lesson, much the way a loving father will administer bad-tasting medicine to an ill and uncomprehending child, knowing full well that true health will eventually result? That precisely was the analogy ministers came to use. God was the author of the apparent dilemma, and for a purpose—to chastise and teach people the futility of forsaking Him and putting too much store in human endeavors like politics and economic opportunism. Once the lesson was learned and the guilty were contrite and asked for forgiveness, a loving God would forgive and send a refreshing revival to reinvigorate religion.

The explanation here briefly summarized required several years to be developed by concerned clergy, and one can follow the halting process of their reasoning through their correspondence and sermons. By the late 1790s the view sketched above had become quite common, and ministers were organizing fast days to indicate to God that their congregation was contrite. In many areas prayer societies were begun to implore God to send the blessing of revival. Once clergy and lay had accepted this explanation for the perceived declension and had taken active steps to right themselves with God, they confidently expected providential intervention to rescue the fortunes of religion. The decade that had begun with ministerial despair had evolved into a period of hopeful anticipation. No one presumed to know precisely when or where God would effect a change for the better, but that deliverance was thought to be imminent. From Virginia to Georgia to Kentucky, this progression from ministerial depression to ministerial expectation was common, and of course their congregations heard these views expressed.[7]

By the end of the eighteenth century the South was primed for a significant period of church growth—the prerequisites for revival were in place, the intellectual climate was prepared. The spark that ignited the region was an outbreak of intense religious frenzy in south-central Kentucky in the summer of 1800. Why there, and why then? Even though the social-cultural conditions were suitable, a fortuitous combination of men and events actually began the small revival that catalyzed the South and produced imitative revivals across the region. The Reverend James McGready, a man of imposing size, piercing eyes, and penetrating voice, sponsored the church service that witnessed the first unusual portents of spiritual renewal.

Born in North Carolina in 1758 and educated to the Presbyterian ministry in Pennsylvania by two ministers who were sons of the First Great Awakening, McGready had passed through Vir-

ginia in 1788 on his way home to North Carolina after ordination
in Pennsylvania. At that moment central Virginia was ablaze with
the mid-1780s revival discussed above, and McGready was especially impressed with a student revival he saw while visiting
Hampden-Sydney College, a revival skillfully stoked by the college president, Presbyterian minister James Blair Smith. Had
McGready needed to be convinced of the efficacy of revival
preaching, his sojourn in Virginia provided the proof. Arriving
thereafter in north-central North Carolina, McGready launched
a hard-hitting campaign of sermons against extravagance and
worldliness, but to little effect. His earnestness inspired several
young men to enter the ministry and some persons in local
churches were moved by his passion, but North Carolina was as
embroiled in politics and expansion as the rest of the South.
Despite McGready's efforts, the general state of religion suffered. McGready responded with harsher attacks on what he saw
as the evils of the age, which only angered those hungry for
slaves and profits. The conflict worsened, until a ransacked
church and a death threat written in blood on the pulpit persuaded McGready that perhaps he should seek another portion of
the Lord's vineyard to cultivate. In the winter of 1795–96 he
followed earlier parishioners who had migrated to Logan County,
Kentucky, a rambunctious frontier area.

By hard experience, then, McGready knew the "declension" in
religion, and he, too, believed that it was a chastisement of God
that would be lifted only when a contrite people prayed for forgiveness and for a renewal of religious vitality. Shortly after taking leadership of three tiny congregations in Kentucky,
McGready convinced many of his people to organize themselves
into prayer societies, imploring God to send spiritual refresh-
ment. At first there were few signs of religious vitality, but
McGready was both determined and patient—and he expected
eventually to see a vigorous resurgence of religion. His hope was
contagious, and by 1799 increasing numbers of members in his
three churches expected someday, perhaps soon, to witness bet-

ter times. One June weekend in 1800, as members from the trio
of churches were meeting together for a series of religious services that were to culminate with communion, two visiting ministers who were brothers—one a Presbyterian McGready had converted back in North Carolina, the other a Methodist—asked to
participate. McGready, knowing the one, agreed. The Friday
evening and Saturday services went as expected, but on Saturday
night the Methodist evangelist rose and began to preach, then,
overcome with emotion, he began to shout and cry, exclaiming
that he felt God's presence at that moment with special
vividness. The normally sedate Presbyterian congregation was
astounded at his emotional outburst and somewhat confused,
when suddenly, at the back of the church, a woman began to
shout and cry. Like an electrical shock excitement swept through
the congregation, and as McGready stood back in amazement,
the whole congregation was caught up in a paroxysm of religious
fervor.

McGready sensed immediately that this remarkable scene was
the sign that the long prayed for, long expected providential
deliverance had begun. Interpreting this event as a minor miracle, the moment the Sunday services were over and the people
had left for home, he began planning another sacramental meeting. Striking while the iron was hot, he sent word to neighboring
congregations of a July 1800 communion service, asking persons
to bring food and shelter so they could simply wait for another
miraculous visitation of the Spirit to occur. One can imagine the
impact this invitation and rumors of what had happened in June
had on curious and expectant Christians in southern Kentucky
and northern Tennessee. As the July date approached, hundreds
of laypersons and almost two dozen ministers from various denominations made preparations to come to McGready's Gasper
River Presbyterian Church. Moreover, hundreds of persons not
belonging to any church were just as curious. Several thousand
attended the event, which—with an unprecedented crowd
camped under the trees, several ministers preaching at once

from makeshift stands, and the smoke of campfires mingling with
the babble of sounds and the multitude of faces—truly seemed
like a God-sent event to lonely backcountry folk who ached for
the sense of religious community they associated with former
homes across the mountains to the east. They were primed to
expect a miracle. Caught up in the heady excitement, many
worshippers were overcome with emotion and fainted, cried,
became hysterial—behavior that seemed in its novelty to confirm
the popular belief that this was a miraculous occasion. Huge
numbers came expecting and wanting to experience a miracle,
and they interpreted the size of the crowd and the fervor of the
services to be proof of what they hoped for.

Like a self-fulfilling prophecy, the Gasper River meeting gal-
vanized churchpeople in the region into vigorous activity, and as
news spread of events in Logan County, emboldened ministers
elsewhere announced the long anticipated revival had com-
menced and scheduled massive outdoor religious services themselves. These outdoor revivals, soon called camp meetings, accommodated crowds far larger than the church buildings could
have handled, and they further suggested the novel religious
forces at work. The pace of religious activity quickly accelerated,
with rumors of success feeding more feverish efforts to hold
meetings and preach. Camp meetings spread across the entire
South, ministers and devout laypersons—exhilarated by the
prospects—preached with energy and effectiveness, and the
Great Revival was in full swing. Given its geographical extent, its
interdenominational appeal, the intensity of religious fervor, and
the numbers of persons added to the church rolls (membership
doubled and tripled in some areas), this was the South's First
Great Awakening.[8]

After 1805 the Great Revival receded, but the die had been
cast. The three evangelical churches—Baptists, Methodists, and
Presbyterians—had been tremendously strengthened, with
membership up significantly and hundreds of young men at-

tracted to the ministry. Their theological interpretation of the
dilemma of the 1790s apparently justified by recent events, the
ministers approached the future filled with confidence. Theological distinctions between the denominations had been submerged during the revival in the desire to win converts, and
although minor disputes arose in the future, theological precision
was deemed irrelevant because shared beliefs seemed so much
more important in the face of threatening deism and indifference. What seemed essential was winning souls, not arguing over
details. Preaching was aimed more at practical results than
philosophical sophistication.

In the absence of major theological disputes and with popular
support high, the Baptists and Methodists in particular were well
positioned for substantial church growth. The camp meeting
proved to be a remarkably effective recruitment technique for
the Methodists (the Presbyterians and to an extent the Baptists
retreated from them for a while because they were deemed too
emotional). Within a decade the camp meeting had become an
accepted human instrumentality for gaining converts, seen no
longer as an unpredictable, God-sent, miraculous event but a
regularly scheduled occasion for preaching, singing, socializing,
and conversion. Camp meeting grounds were established, with
semipermanent preaching stands and tent sites. In towns the
camp meeting was adapted to different needs, and in the form of
the "protracted meeting"—utilizing churches, homes for prayer
groups, and perhaps a visiting preacher—the annual revival became part of the community routine. With the rise of Sunday
Schools, the proliferation of religious literature, and clergy-
taught schools, academies, and even colleges, the cultural dominance in the South of evangelical Protestantism was practically
complete by the third decade of the nineteenth century.[9]

While expanding from a despised, at times persecuted minority in 1770 to a comfortable majority position in 1820, the
evangelical churches also broadened their class appeal. Popular

at first in regions where the aristocratic and Anglican establishment was weakest and appealing to those who felt rejected by the
ruling elite, the evangelicals prescribed a life-style greatly at
variance with that of the slaveocracy. The evangelical ideal of
simplicity and humility was in part a conscious rejection of the
dominant values they did not have the wherewithal to emulate,[10]
and a rendering into practice of principles garnered from the
New Testament and borrowed from New England (Separate Baptist) and Old England (Wesleyan) forebearers.[11] Their life-style
that seemed such a rebuke to the ostentation and arrogance of
the colonial elite made them appear an ominous threat, and
hence the evangelicals were ridiculed and mistreated by the ruling authorities. But as the evangelicals grew in numbers and
influence, gaining converts from the middling sort as well as the
backcountry poor, they gradually became more familiar, less
threatening, and more acceptable.

The Presbyterians, with their tradition of learned ministers
and orderly services, quite easily made the transition from out-
cast to acceptance, and even the Baptists and Methodists—their
defensiveness lessening in the aftermath of revival successes and
their demeanor improving as their appeal broadened—came
soon to be seen as members of society, not cultural insurgents.
Now and then in the late colonial period a wealthy planter would
convert to either the Baptist or Methodist faith, a conversion the
evangelicals made much of. This tendency of gaining upper-class
converts was greatly accelerated by the Great Revival, so much
so that in many (especially newer) areas the local planter aristo-
crats were more likely to be Baptists or Methodists than Episcopalians. Even in Jefferson's Virginia by the second decade of
the nineteenth century, evangelical views had become so prevalent that those of the aristocracy who had not joined the Baptists,
Methodists, or Presbyterians had seen their own Episcopal
church adopt many of the sentimental, evangelical emphases of
the popular churches.[12] To a remarkable degree, evangelical religion shaped the mentalité of antebellum southerners, rich and

poor, slaveholder and nonslaveholder. By 1830 the "Solid South" was more a religious than a political reality.[13]

The evangelical hegemony represented a significant shift from colonial days, but the result was less a sense of religious community than a religious culture, to make an important distinction. During the late colonial period, in those regions where there was an established church, everyone was presumed to occupy a position in a hierarchial community determined by church and civil laws. In that context the evangelicals, with their willingness to preach anywhere at any time and with their alternative values that emphasized self-denying humility, constituted a culturally revolutionary force. Evangelical successes wore away at the cultural dominance of the established church and court, but in their place the evangelicals did not establish a new general community.

Because of their emphasis on individual salvation and the spiritual purity of the individual congregation—maintained through strict church discipline—the evangelicals privatized religion. The central focus of revival converts continued to be individualistic, broadened only to include the fellow members of their congregation. This intense localism strengthed the bond between converts and their home congregation, furthered the moral authority of the congregation working together in disciplinary proceedings, and reinforced the pietistic dimension of southern religion, but little sense of identity with or responsibility for the society beyond the local congregation emerged. Their theology stressed rejecting worldliness, not remaking the world. The evangelicals tended to be otherwordly; they showed scant willingness to address social or moral conditions beyond the immediate realm of their own congregation, in part because of an overreaction to the perceived faults of the Anglican establishment in colonial times. Reforming individual sinners was their emphasis, and the ills of society they saw as less a legitimate social concern than the aggregate sins of numerous individuals. Hence further evangelicalism, not societal criticism or "reform," was their prescription.[14] The kind of social perfectionism associated with Charles G. Finney and northern revivalism was alien to southern evangelicalism.

However, the felt necessity of defending slavery in order to salvage a role for themselves in society led evangelicals into involvement with the "world" in a conservative way drastically at odds with northern revivalism, which was in close alliance with abolitionism. In the opening decades of the evangelical presence in the South, when they were outside the community establishment and occupied the bottom rungs of society, Baptists and Methodists welcomed black converts with open arms. Their worship services were integrated, with blacks sitting in the churches (though usually in the back pews or in the balcony), hearing the same sermons, taking communion with whites, participating in church discipline, even occasionally voting, and being buried in the same cemetaries. Seeing blacks as souls to convert, the Baptists and Methodists in their openness to slaves as persons stood as an open rebuke to the planter aristocracy—another reason the politico-religious establishment persecuted the evangelicals.

When the majority of Baptists and Methodists were themselves outside the established community, it was easy for them to recognize the humanity of the bondsmen, the ultimate outsiders. For that very reason many planters feared the consequence of evangelical preaching to slaves, for there was not only the dread of potential rebellion but the worry that Christian slaves were a contradiction in terms—would black Christians try to use their baptism as a grounds for emancipation? As a result, planters restricted evangelicals from preaching to slaves and even threatened their ability to preach to other whites. The Baptists and Methodists, realizing that their stance toward slavery might seriously hamper their ability to spread their version of the gospel, chose to make their racial attitudes conform more closely to the slaveholders' ethos. As Francis Asbury wrote in 1809, noting that "masters are afraid of the influence of our principles": "Would not an *amelioration* in the condition and treatment of slaves have produced more practical good to the poor Africans, than any attempt at their *emancipation?* The state of society, unhappily, does not admit of this: besides, the blacks are deprived of the means of instruction; who will take the pains to lead them into the way of salvation . . . but the Methodists? . . . What is the personal liberty of the African which he may abuse, to the salvation of his soul; how may it be compared?"[15] By compromising with society on the issue of emancipation, the Methodists (and Baptists) would be enabled to bring the gospel of salvation to the slaves. The preachers reasoned that was a good trade off; in exchange for the ability to grow as denominations, the quintessential southern churches gave up their critical stance toward slavery. No longer would it be addressed as a social evil; now it was seen as an inevitable, natural, and hence ordained-by-God part of southern society.

Having to defend slavery in order to have the liberty of spreading their message, the Baptists and Methodists in particular found themselves in effect defending southern society itself. After Nat Turner's insurrection in 1831 and the increasing tension between the sections, to criticise any substantial aspect of southern society was considered tantamount to joining forces with the abolitionists. So the evangelicals, prospering in the South, were hesitant to jeopardize their position; they ended up defending southern society as one especially propitious for Christianity and slavery as a benevolent institution ordained by God for the spiritual improvement of Africans. In one of the great ironies of southern history, the evangelicals who began in the South posed against the slaveholding aristocracy were by the 1830s identifying with southern society and defending it as the most Christian society known to man. By the end of the antebellum period southern evangelicals, who earlier had renounced all responsibility for worldly institutions and values, were proclaiming a Christian social ethic to defend slavery and thereby paternalistically "care" for the souls of the poor Africans entrusted to their stewardship! When, finally, southern evangelicals discovered social responsibility, it was a conservative ethic not to perfect society but to apotheosize slaveholding.[16] Thus Methodist William Winans could speak of being "a slaveholder *on* [Christian] *principle*" and Presbyterian Benjamin Palmer could justify secession on Christian grounds.[17] After the Civil War southern evangelicals returned to their earlier tradition of renouncing responsibility for society and advocated with a vengeance that the only proper concern for the church was the conversion of individuals.

Christian slaveholders were not just being hypocritical when they spoke of slavery as an institution used by God to convert the African heathen. By their lights, and in terms of their experience, Christianization was one of the undeniable results of bondage. Since they in general terms argued that one's position in the eyes of God—that is, being converted—was more important than one's civil state in human society, white Christians could be blind to the immorality of slavery as a social institution when they knew of slaves' individual Christian faith. And no discussion of Protestantism in the Old South is complete without consideration of the presence of black Christians in the region's "white" churches. From the first moment, slaves were members of the evangelical churches, especially the Baptist and Methodist. One finds them, for example, signing (often with an "X") the charters of incorporation, and throughout the period substantial numbers of slaves were on the membership roles.

Although one must never forget that American slavery was a racist institution and the South a racist society, one should also realize that in the churches slaves were treated more nearly as equals than anywhere else in the society.[18] Slaves, for example, participated in the church disciplinary procedures, testifying against whites and speaking on their own behalf in the face of white charges, and black testimony was apparently taken at its worth—this at a time when blacks could not testify against whites in the civil courts of the land. Slaves were held by the whites, and by the slaves themselves, to the same moral code as whites.

Not only did this reinforce the bondsperson's sense of self-worth, but it provided an arena for moral growth and leadership. Blacks were occasionally appointed deacons, were often allowed to preach to mixed audiences, and were addressed in the church records (letters of admission and dismissal) the same as whites: as Brother Jones and Sister Smith, for example.

Evangelical religion offered slaves far more than pie-in-the-sky escapism. It provided a close-knit black community, it provided a sense of moral worth, it provided purpose and direction for life (above and beyond the daily commands of owner or driver), and it gave moments of hope and joy to many whose life otherwise would have been more drab. Slavery was a dehumanizing institution, and one of the slaves' major achievements was discovering a variety of coping mechanisms that enabled them to hold on to their humanity. Their religion—faith and practice—more than any other cultural development, allowed bondspersons to survive slavery with their personhood intact.

To a surprising degree, there was a biracial religious culture in the antebellum South. Whites seldom if ever appreciated how profoundly religion served the slave community, but they did understand that there were many devout slave Christians. That knowledge undergirded one of the major white defenses of the institution, and made whites furious when abolitionists chided southern churchmen for neglecting the souls of the blacks. In the aftermath of abolitionist criticism and after the separation of the southern churches from national organizations guaranteed that southern churches were "safe" on the slavery issue, white churches mounted an extensive "mission to the slaves" that increased religious opportunities for bondspersons. But the black Christian community antedated this campaign by two generations.

To an extent the biracial religious culture ameliorated racial tensions, and certainly it led some whites to see blacks as humans struggling with the evils and temptations of life. Religion also helped minimize class tensions among whites. Wealthy planters went to church with their poorest neighbors everywhere except some aristocratic enclaves like the South Carolina sea islands. Plain folks and wealthy planters sat in the same churches, heard the same sermons, were subject to the same discipline, shared the same theology, and agreed that slavery was ordained by God. Religion as well as racism made possible a white folks democracy in the Old South. By the 1820s evangelicalism was definitely no rebellious force but rather a pillar of the establishment. This is not to deny that many whites felt, consciously and unconsciously, vague feelings of guilt over slaveholding—especially when they knew the institution was not being practiced as humanely as it might be—and evangelicalism offered an escape from guilt. An emphasis on personal wrongdoing and sin and the promise of God's forgiveness were at the heart of evangelicalism; for many white southerners one of the primary functions of their religion was absolution for their failings. Revivals and camp meetings served this purpose, for most people who confessed and promised a rededication of their lives at these meetings were already church members. The heady emotionalism of the revival service was a way of purging guilt and reinforcing faith through a public ceremony.

Slaves were not the only subordinate group for whom evangelical religion provided meaning, purpose, an enhanced awareness of self-worth, and an arena for leadership and self-development denied in the larger society. Southern white women played an extremely important role in the lives of the churches, and conversely the churches played an extremely important role in the lives of the women.[19] Women made up a disproportionate percentage of church membership; ministers depended on them being in place each Sunday filling the pews and staffing Sunday Schools; there were women's prayer societies, women's auxiliaries, and sewing societies; women utilized various means to raise money for all kinds of church projects and participated in the committee structure of the churches. In the First Baptist Church of Galveston, Texas, for example, women during the antebellum period were appointed to a pew committee to solicit pew rents, they served on a special Committee of Discipline to monitor the conduct of several backslidden sisters, they hosted an ice-cream social to raise money to purchase a church bell, and their Baptist Sewing Society contributed funds for the pastor's salary.[20] Although there was probably no self-conscious women's culture, women, excluded from active participation in politics and the professions, found the church their sphere for personal development. It was assumed women were somehow naturally religious and nurturing. At times of childbirth, sickness, and death, women who knew each other at church came to the assistance of one another. For women often lonely on their plantations or isolated small farms, the church offered fellowship (or sorority) and an opportunity to work for charitable and other purposes outside their home. Clearly neither white women nor black slaves were treated as the absolute equals of white males—white women, for example, were obviously subordinate in authority to the males who technically governed the churches. Yet women's active and substantial roles in the churches in the antebellum South must be compared not with today's norms but with their circumscribed position in the larger society of that time. Emphasizing the victimization of antebellum southern white women without respecting the many ways their church life gave them important goals to work for and a sense of social importance is to seriously misunderstand the reality of southern womanhood.

Evangelical religion was an essential component of southern life and culture for bond and free, male and female. Through the immediate fellowship of the local congregation it provided a community to belong to, it mediated tensions between the races and the classes, it made life seem less inexplicable and tragedy more acceptable, and it provided an initial building block for southern identity and eventual southern nationalism. For us in a more secular age it is often difficult to take seriously the expressed religious values of people many generations removed. But to quote C. Vann Woodward in a slightly different context, "The modern reader would do well to keep in mind that the gulf between him and [those with different values who came before] is not necessarily one of intelligence or charity or sophistication, but of time. And if one cannot bridge that gulf he is cut off from a great many worthies who are not his contemporaries."[21] Studying southern evangelical religion fairly and with all the sensitivity one can muster provides a unique window through which to observe antebellum southern culture with its nuances, subtleties, and apparent contradictions.

The Black Heritage
in Religion in the South

C. ERIC LINCOLN

The Unchangeable Will of God

During the summer of 1619, twenty Africans held captive aboard
a Dutch frigate were turned over to the English colonists at
Jamestown, Virginia, in exchange for provisions for the ship's
crew. This event marked the beginning of the black experience
with English America and American Christianity. Actually, the
African experience in America antedated that of the English by at
least a hundred years, for thousands of Africans had served with
the Spanish conquistadores in their sixteenth-century odyssey of
exploration and conquest that stretched from Peru to what is now
Florida, Arizona, and New Mexico. Some of these Africans were
undoubtedly Christian, but enough of them were "Moors" or
Muslims to cause the Spanish crown to take strong measures
against their attempts to plant Islam among the Indians.[1]

African Muslims were also identified from time to time among
the slaves brought by the English colonists two centuries later.
However, because the religious inclinations of the slaves were
dismissed as either nonexistent or heathen, no records were
kept. Except for a few extant legends referring to occasional
Muslims who somehow managed to impress their masters with
their religious fidelity in spite of their enslavement, the full story
of the Islamic presence in English America is yet to be developed. A recent study claims that as many as 20 percent of the
Africans involuntarily settled in America were Muslims and suggests the magnitude of what is still unknown about the religions
of the slaves.[2]

By the middle of the seventeenth century the brisk trade in African slaves had reached America from the Carribean and the indentured servitude system, which had provided the principal source of labor in the colonies, gave way to institutionalized black slavery. As the legal term for the holding of Africans crystallized into *dura vita*, their numbers increased rapidly, and religion was increasingly defined and expressed in consonance with the economic and political interests of the planters who claimed them as property. In consequence, little occasion arose and less opportunity existed for serious black involvement in Christianity until the advent of the "Great Awakening" in the 1730s. Indeed, by the end of the sixteenth century, with very minor exceptions, the "religion" of the black diaspora was limited for the most part to what could be remembered of African ritual and belief and adapted to plantation life and culture. From the beginning many planters determined the Africans to be either unworthy of Christianity or incapable of it. This determination was buttressed by the fear that to Christianize the slaves would threaten the very carefully developed master-servant relationship, and worse than that, directly jeopardize the property interest the planters claimed in their chattels, for the legal questions surrounding Christians holding their brothers-in-Christ as slaves were still untested and still unresolved.

Breaking Down the Barriers

Around 1701 the Society for the Propagation of the Gospel in Foreign Parts, a missionary arm of the Anglican church organized to convert the Indians, began to petition the planters to permit the proselytization of their slaves. The SPG argued that even though the Africans' lowly status in this life was ordained of God, their souls were still as precious as any others. Beyond that, the argument ran, it was in the planters' best interest for blacks to be brought to Christ, for if the slaves were properly imbued with the principles of Christian love and morality they would make more reliable servants, less given to spite and malingering, and they would be more content with their plight knowing it to be the unchangeable will of God. The Bishop of London issued letters denying that the confession of Christianity would affect the earthly status of the slaves in any way, and the colonial legislatures gave legal confirmation to this ecclesiastical assurance. So it was that almost a hundred years after they first arrived at Jamestown the way was tentatively opened for blacks to have a kind of auxillary status in American Christianity. Neither the planters nor their slaves were much impressed with this accomplishment in the beginning. For the planters, whatever the alleged benefits of owning Christian slaves, troublesome risks had also to be considered. Religious instruction and worship services required time—time off from work or time garnered from the rest the slaves needed to sustain them in the fields. Further, religious instruction might be abused as a cover for the plotting of insurrection; or it could lead to difficult questions about the master–slave relationship. Even more threatening was the possibility that such instruction might somehow result in blacks learning how to read, an attainment considered most inimical to the control and maintenance of slavery.

In 1715 a North Carolina law forbade "any master or owner of Negroes or slaves . . . [to permit them] . . . to build . . . any meeting house upon account of worship . . ."[3] And in 1800 a South Carolina statute made it unlawful for ". . . slaves, free Negroes, mulattoes or mestigoes, even in the company of white persons to . . . assemble for the purpose of religious worship, either before the rising of the sun, or the going down of the same."[4] Other laws forbade blacks to preach except to their own families, barred blacks from preaching altogether; or required that from five to a majority of whites be present at any worship service blacks could attend.

As for the slaves, most of those on the larger plantations were so effectively removed from Christian contact as to be unaware of what was at stake. In the towns and cities opportunities to experience the white man's faith were somewhat less remote, but the blacks who had a chance to observe Christian practices at close range were often puzzled by what they saw, and they were not always convinced that their conversion to the faith was worth the effort. Even in New England, black involvement in the Christian churches was the infrequent exception and not the rule. As late as 1780 Governor Bradstreet wrote that of the blacks in Massachusetts there were "none baptized as far as I ever heard of." During the same period Dean Berkeley of Rhode Island said that his parishoners "considered the Blacks as creatures of another species who had no rights to be admitted to the sacraments." This, he added, "was the main obstacle to the conversion of these poor people."

A convocation of Anglican ministers meeting at Oxford, Maryland, in 1731 concluded that though the white Christians "allow [the religious instructions of blacks] to be a good thing, yet they generally excuse themselves as thinking it to be impractical," or "they will not be of any pains and troubles of it." But one clergyman, a Mr. Fletcher, confessed that his parishoners were "generally so brutish they they would not suffer their Negroes to be instructed, catechized, nor baptized. . . ."[6] All these reasons and others were buttressed by a pervasive folklore, which held blacks to be "too dull" to be instructed, or "without souls," or otherwise incapable of Christian responsibility.

Sharing the Gospel

Determining with exactness the point at which the unconcern and rejection of the general Christian community began to abate is difficult. But in spite of a climate that was originally unreceptive, Christianity did eventually establish deep roots in the black subculture, and there it became the organizing matrix of the black experience.

The church in colonial America was essentially an experience of the privileged classes, and although the general status of the blacks, both slave and free, was considerably more distressed than that of others, they were not alone in their exclusion from organized religion. But by the turn of the eighteenth century, orthodoxy was in serious decline in America, and by 1740 reform centered in a series of soul-searching revivals was on the move throughout the colonies. Like thousands of whites who found themselves outside the formal structures of the established churches, large numbers of blacks were caught suddenly in the fervor of this "Great Awakening." In the camp meetings and brush arbors where rousing preaching and fervent singing and praying loosed the spirit and unshackled the emotions, they lost themselves in an inner freedom, which was beyond the command of the master and the lash of the overseer. The powerful preaching of the tireless evangelists who traveled from camp to camp and of the occasional black "exhorters" who were from time to time permitted to share their gifts of the spirit made religion an available option for the blacks (and for many poor whites) for the first time.

In the camp meetings the status differences between black and white, or master and slave, were seldom rigidly observed, much to the consternation of the parish clergy who generally scorned the informal outdoor services and the men who led them as well. The church pastors were usually men of extensive theological training, and they were particularly annoyed by the occasional spectale of blacks in the role of preachers. One minister complained that "the very servants and slaves pretend to extraordinary inspiration, and under the veil thereof . . . run rambling about to utter enthusiastic nonescnse."[7] Another divine was even more outraged to discover that "Negroes [had] even taken upon themselves the business of preaching."

Though the camp meetings of the First Great Awakening provided the impetus for black involvement in American Christianity, they were a transient phenomenon outside the mainstream of institutionalized religion. Ultimately, the sustaining force of that involvement depended upon other opportunities including those presented by the institutional church.

Planters discovered that substantial benefits could indeed be derived from turning the "heathen" blacks, who were often considered surly and unpredictable, into Christians motivated with the desire to merit God's favor through service to the masters he had set over them. Slaveowners were considerably less hostile, then, to the notion of having a Christianized servile class among them. The chief obstacle was to insure that the version of the faith available to the slaves was always consistent with the critical objectives of slavery. In consequence, a number of strategies emerged designed to Christianize the Africans without burdening them with those principles of the gospel likely to prove unsettling or in conflict with the realities of their status in this life. Often the slaveholder or his wife assumed the responsibility of teaching and catechizing those blacks in attendance on them at the "Big House." On the smaller plantations, even the field hands might be assembled under the magnolias of the Big House compound to hear the master or the mistress read selectively from the Bible and explain God's will regarding the slaves and their moral obligations. In some instances, the task of spiritual mentor was even delegated to the overseer with no apparent sense of role conflict.

A few large plantations had resident preachers, who as part and parcel of the manorial arrangement were charged with the religious interests of the whole plantation and responsible to the master for whatever was preached or taught and for its effect upon the slaves. As time passed some of the most effective plantation preachers were slaves who learned enough approved scripture and doctrine from the white preachers and adapted it to their own interpretative style and delivery to develop large followings among the blacks and often among the whites as well. One of the more celebrated black preachers of this genre was George Liele of Virginia. Liele was converted by a white Baptist preacher sometime before the Revolution and soon after began to preach. So impressed was his master with his gifts, and most especially with the salutary effect his preaching had on his fellow bondsmen, that Liele was given his freedom and permitted to pursue his ministry full time. He gained much attention as a preacher in South Carolina and later migrated to Kingston, Jamaica, where in 1784 he organized the first Baptist church in Jamaica.

Another southern black preacher noted for his ministry among the slaves was a Baptist preacher affectionately known as "Uncle Jack." Uncle Jack too converted blacks and whites alike as he preached on the Virginia plantations. In his old age he was rewarded with his freedom and a small farm. A similar honor was declined by George Bently who pastored a racially mixed plantation-based congregation in Tennessee, because he felt his ministry could be more effectively maintained under the protection and support of his master.

Although some alternatives existed, the most typical method of spiritual nurture for the plantation population was the occasional visits of missionaries, itinerant preachers, and exhorters, all of whom were routinely white. The message they brought was designed to reinforce the existing arrangements between master and slave by invoking the scriptures as sacred proof that these arrangements were ordained by God. A sermon directed to the slaves by a Virginia cleric declared in part:

> Almighty God hath been pleased to make you slaves here, and to give you nothing but labor and poverty in this world, which you are obliged to submit to as it is His will. . . . If therefore, you would be God's freemen in Heaven, you must be good and strive to serve him here on earth. I say that what faults you are guilty of towards your masters and mistresses are faults done against God Himself, who hath set (them) over you in His own stead. . . . leave your cause in the hands of God: He will reward you for it in heaven. . . .[8]

Or as a popular ditty put it, "Work and pray, live on hay, you'll have pie in the sky when you die!"

By 1840 the missionary movement among the slaves had the support of most of the denominational churches. The Methodists were most zealous, closely seconded by the Baptists, with the

Presbyterians and Episcopalians active but less prominent in the plantation ministry. In theory, the missionary movement aimed considerably beyond the mere spiritual accommodation of the slaves to their unhappy fate. It sought to offer the planters a much more challenging motivation for Christianizing the blacks: the humanization of both slave and master. The missionary organizations proposed regular Sunday preaching to the slaves, ideally attended by master and mistress. These were to be augmented by evening meetings, oral instruction, catechizing, and by whatever additional efforts might be needed for effective Christian nurture. But in spite of the zeal of the missionaries, preaching to the slaves was generally considered by most white clergymen to be a contemptible ministry, if not an actual abuse of the calling. Although missionaries were willing to offer themselves for the dubious assignment, both the planters and the sponsoring churches were wary, and the missionary ideal never developed into a significant spiritual enterprise. The reluctance of the planters was aggravated by at least three major slave insurrections, beginning with that led by Gabriel Prosser in 1800. Two of them (led by Denmark Vesey in 1822 and Nat Turner in 1831) had overt religious overtones. Moreover, the constant abolitionist agitation from the North challenged the morality of slavery and made any religious instruction to the slaves potentially hazardous. But in spite of these problems by the outbreak of the Civil War about a quarter of a million blacks were in the southern wing of the Methodist church, and almost twice as many were Baptists.

In The White Man's Church

Religious services on the plantation were as infrequent as once a month, and few plantations had their own churches or meetinghouses. In the cities and towns, a scattering of black churches (mostly Baptist) dated back to the early nineteenth century. However, until the fracture of American Protestantism brought on by the Civil War, the prevailing custom was for white and black Christians to worship in the same white church, usually attending the same services. Blacks in attendance were both slave and free, but all Africans were treated as one servile class. The slave contingent most often included Big House slaves or personal servants, along with certain plantation-based slaves who were permitted to hire their own time in the cities. Then there were the numerous servants and artisans who lived in the cities and towns, which depended upon them for ordinary labor and professional services. Included in this class were barbers, engineers, iron workers, plasterers, waiters, bricklayers, coach drivers, grooms, etc.

Some blacks were permitted to hold attenuated memberships in the white churches, but the prevailing custom was to separate the two races during worship services. In some cases the black members were restricted to services designed especially for them and held before or after the regular services attended by whites. Where simultaneous worship was permitted, blacks were restricted to segregated seating on special benches placed around the perimeter of the sanctuary or to the rear of all white worshippers. If the black membership exceeded these arrangements, as was frequently the case, special galleries or "nigger heavens" might be constructed at the rear of the sanctuary for their accommodation. Often these galleries and the rear seating arrangements for blacks on the main floor were screened so as to effectively shut them from the view of the white worshippers. If these measures proved insufficient, the blacks who longed to share the faith had but small recourse. The minutes of the Presbyterian Synod for South Carolina and Georgia meeting in 1834 illustrates their dilemma. The minutes declare that:

> The gospel, as things are now can never be preached to the two classes successfully in conjunction. The galleries or the back seats on the lower floors of white churches are generally appropriated to the Negroes, when it can be done without inconveniences to the whites. When it cannot be done conve-

niently, the Negroes must catch the gospel as it escapes through the doors and windows.[9]

In spite of such inconveniences, the black membership at times exceeded the white church enrollment. For example, in 1827 the South Carolina Conference of the Methodist Church reported a membership of 46,000, almost exactly one-third of whom were black. In 1860, of the 86,000 members reported by the Conference, more than 48,000, or about 56 percent, were black.

Black members could not participate in the business or deliberations of the church or hold office, although some churches would occasionally permit a black exhorter to preach. Black members could not be offered holy communion until every white person had been served. Some ministers gave special attention to their black parishioners, reserving a part of their sermons to treat the subjects considered especially appropriate to them, and delivering the sermon in simply language designed for their understanding. Other pastors refused to acknowledge the presence of blacks in any way on the grounds that merely being among white Christians was itself sufficiently uplifting for them; they regarded it as the responsibility of their owners or others interested in their spiritual welfare to interpret to the blacks the message God had intended for a white constituency.

The Invisible Church

Despite the frustrations they suffered in the white churches, many black Christians faithfully maintained attendance and endeavored to find in the faith the spiritual salvation promised them. Others were less patient, and some entertained the most serious doubts about the Christian enterprise as they experienced it. Lunsford Lane, an exslave from Raleigh, North Carolina, recalls his ambivalence regarding the white church he attended:

I was permitted to attend church, and this I esteem a great blessing. It was there that I received much instruction, which I trust was a great benefit . . . [but] there was one hard doctrine to which we . . . were compelled to listen, which I found difficult to receive. We were often told by the ministers how much we owed to God for bringing us over from the benighted shores of Africa and permitting us to listen to the sound of the gospel. In ignorance of any special revelation that God had made to [the white man] or to his ancestors, that my ancestors should be stolen and enslaved on the soil of America to accomplish their salvation, I was slow to believe all my teachers enjoined on this subject. Many of us left (the church), considering like the doubting disciple of old: this is a hard saying; who can hear it?[10]

Black Christians were most often discouraged by the hasty reversion of their white brothers and sisters in Christ to more familiar roles once the benediction had been said and the church doors had swung shut. Disappointment was at least partly responsible for the popular belief that Christian masters, not excluding slave-owning preachers, were often "harder" than those without religious pretentions. Whatever their reasons, and undoubtedly there were many, not all black believers were content to seek their spiritual fulfillment in the white man's church. Black churches were everywhere proscribed or closely monitored, and clandestine religious meetings always posed the risk of floggings by the "pattyrollers," who were the citizens charged with the apprehension and punishment of any slave found abroad without a written pass of permission. A slave also risked being sold away from family and friends if discovered. Yet, secret religious gatherings were common up to the Civil War, and they involved enough slaves and free blacks to constitute a substantial underground church. This "Invisible Church" met deep in the woods and swamps, as far as possible from the suspicious eyes of the master or his overseer. At these clandestine religious services, wild game or as often as not pigs taken from the plantation pig lots were roasted over hot coals carefully spread in a pit to avoid telltale smoke and flame that would bring down the overseer or the "pattyrollers." The roasted meat was carefully seasoned with wild herbs found in abundance in the forests, and convention has it that this was the origin of the southern tradition of "barbecue." There in the security of the wilderness the black worshippers assembled around a large iron pot, inverted to capture the sound of the fervent preaching, praying, and singing, which marked the style of the Invisible Church.

The religious underground was led by black preachers whose prime credentials were a "call" from God and whose principal learning was mother wit. Yet, this invisible institution flourished as the most satisfying alternative to the perplexities of the white church. In the Invisible Church there were no "masters" and no "mistresses," and God ordained no special punishment or subservience for black people. The Invisible Church drew its membership primarily from the field slaves who were less accommodated than other slaves to the white man's way of life and less susceptible to his spiritual reasoning. Nevertheless, leadership in the Invisible Church was often supplied by slaves from the Big House, by free blacks who had gained a knowledge of the Bible in the white churches, or from itinerant white preachers and missionaries (although slaves did not succumb to their peculiar interpretations of the faith). The genius of these preachers lay in their ability to adapt what they had learned to the existing needs and circumstances of their people and to transpose the white man's message of subservient obedience into a confident awareness that things were not as they should be, or as they would be. There would come a day when "Ethiopia shall stretch forth her hands. . . ." In the meantime, the Invisible Church became an important staging area for escape to freedom in this world as well as in the world to come. It was often the first station on the Underground Railroad, providing cover and information and encouragement for slaves who elected to run away to the North. But for those who remained in bondage, it contributed substantially to the self–esteem that made survival possible, and hope something more than fantasy. Above all, the Invisible Church provided concrete experience in risk and responsibility, both spiritual and practical, and at the highest level. It proved under the most adverse circumstances possible the black capacity for responsible self-determination.

Separate Black Churches and the Development of Black Denominations

The common rule was to deny black Christians the privilege of independent churches, but notable exceptions to the rule existed. The primary concern in the proscription of black churches was, of course, to reduce the risk of plots of insurrection that might be hatched under cover of religion. But this motivation was strongly reinforced by the need to believe that the moral and philosophical aspects of the faith were quite beyond the capacity of black people to understand or to honor except under white tutelege. Besides, there was no organized or trained black clergy, and little prospect of any. Perhaps even more compelling was the general unwillingness to risk the desecration or the distortion of the faith in the hands of the untutored African, or worse, to instruct him and ordain him at the risk of challenging established social conventions or violating the civil law, which was carefully designed to exclude him from most of the amenities and the responsibilities of the Atlantic experiment. But Christianity does not readily lend itself to selective allocation, for its values are most fully realized when they are most freely shared. Moreover, exposure to a little religion is for the spiritually hungry the most certain catalyst to an ever larger experience. It was inevitable that some white Christians would ignore conventional bounds of propriety in the interest of black Christianity. No less inevitably some blacks would want to experience for themselves the full range of Christian endeavor, including the development of their own churches.

The first black church in America is thought to have been a Baptist church established between 1750 and 1773 at Silver Bluff, South Carolina. In the 1770s its pastor was David George, a slave who had been converted by Wait Palmer, a white Baptist preacher. At least two other early churches grew out of the church at Silver Bluffs. They were Springfield Baptist Church at Augusta, Georgia, founded in 1783, and the First African Baptist Church of Savannah, organized in 1785. In 1776 the Harrison Street Church was organized at Petersburg, Virginia, as was another Baptist church in Williamsburg. By 1822 thirty-seven black Baptist churches existed in America, and all but seven were in the South. However, the increasing tensions brought on by northern abolitionist fervor and the fear of black insurrection sharply reduced the growth of separate black churches in the South thereafter. At the close of the Civil War, the number of black Baptist churches in the North had increased to thirty-eight, whereas the number south of the Mason-Dixon Line still stood at thirty. In time, the black Baptists would form three major denominations: The National Baptist Convention, USA (1880); The National Baptist Convention of America (1915); and The Progressive National Baptist Convention (1961). Together they represented the largest body of black Baptists in the world.

The Baptists were more prolific in the establishment of separate black churches, but the Methodists were first to form a national black church or denomination. Black Christians were a prominent part of American Methodism from its inception. In 1766, in New York City, among the five people who gathered to hear a Methodist preacher, and who later formed the first Methodist Society in America, was a black woman named "Betty." The Society grew and eventually established the John Street Methodist Church, the "mother church" of Methodism. Several blacks are named among those who contributed to the fund for building John Street, and by 1795 at least 155 of its members were black. The rapid spread of Methodism throughout America was in no small part attributable to its singular appeal to blacks and to the eagerness of the Methodist preachers, both white and black, to evangelize them. The Methodist church developed a pronounced opposition to slavery quite early, but was unable to realize its antislavery commitments in the face of the overwhelming opposition confronting it in the South where its membership was concentrated. Inevitably, the prevailing contagion of segregation and denigration of black members became standard practice in the Methodist church, and just as inevitably, black Methodists sought relief in a church of their own.

The precipitating incident occurred in 1787 at St. George's Methodist Church in Philadelphia when some black members were dragged from their knees while at prayer in a segregated church gallery. Led by Richard Allen, many of the blacks withdrew from St. George's and in 1894 established a church of their own, Bethel African Methodist Episcopal Church. The founding of Bethel was closely followed by the establishment of Zion Chapel in New York City, where the black members of the John Street Methodist Church also felt compelled to withdraw because of segregationist policies. Zion became mother church to a second black denomination, The African Methodist Episcopal Church Zion. In 1786 and 1887 black members withdrew from two other historic white Methodist churches, Centennial and Lovely Lane of Baltimore. Once again the issue was segregation. After meeting separately from house to house for ten years, the two groups of black spiritual refugees joined in founding Bethel Methodist Church in Baltimore in 1797. Other black Methodists with similar experiences founded churches in Attleboro, Pennsylvania; Wilmington, Delaware; and Salem, New Jersey, in eloquent protest of their unwillingness to participate in the profanation of the faith through the segregation of its brotherhood.

Survival of the separated black Methodist churches proved quite difficult. Unlike the Baptists, Methodism is a "connectional" church and all church properties are controlled or owned by the annual conferences, which are subdivisions of the corporate church or denominational body. Only ordained ministers may hold membership in the annual conference, and no blacks were ordained in the Methodist church until 1829 (although some were licensed as "exhorters" or "local preachers"). As a result, not only did the all-white annual conferences claim the power to appoint pastors to all Methodist churches in their jurisdictions, they also laid claim to all property belonging to churches calling themselves Methodist, black churches included. In consequence, the struggle for full freedom from the control of the segregated white Methodist church went on for two decades or more.

Most of the members of the separated black Methodist churches were free blacks anxious to add to the narrow ambit of their freedom the realization of personhood, including the responsibility for their own spiritual welfare. In 1816 at a call from Richard Allen, representatives from seven black Methodist churches in five states along the Middle Atlantic seaboard met in Philadelphia and organized the African Methodist Episcopal Church denomination. Allen was elected bishop, and the black church as an organized entity had come into being.

In 1821, with six churches from New York, Connecticut, and Pennsylvania, led by Zion Chapel (which was organized by the John Street dissidents), the African Methodist Episcopal Zion Church became a denominational body. James Varick was elected its first bishop in 1822.

The third black Methodist denomination grew directly out of the Methodist Episcopal Church South, which split from the (national) Methodist Episcopal Church over the issue of slavery in 1844. Boasting 207,000 black members before the Civil War, the Methodist church in the South could count only 78,000 when the war was over. A principal catalyst for the drastic erosion of black membership was the crusading zeal of the independent African churches (AME and AMEZ), whose missionaries followed close on the heels of the Union armies as they occupied the southern towns and plantations. The African churches were the first concrete symbols of the black man's freedom and independence, and the blacks left the southern white churches *en masse* to identify with their own. Alarmed by the defection of its black membership, the southern Methodists at their general conference in 1866 decided that, because it was not convenient to change the conventional arrangements for blacks in the white church, the black Methodists would be permitted to organize their own churches if they so desired, with the hope that they would continue at some other level their historic fraternal bonds in Christ with their erstwhile masters.

A substantial number of blacks "so desired," and in four years there were enough black churches whose members were formerly of the Methodist Episcopal Church South to constitute eight annual (or local) conferences in Tennessee, Arkansas, Georgia, Kentucky, Texas, Alabama, South Carolina, and Mississippi. Representatives of these conferences met at Jackson, Tennessee, in a general conference presided over by Senior Bishop Robert Paine of the (white) Methodist Episcopal Church South, and established the third black Methodist denomination, the CME, or Colored Methodist Episcopal Church in America (renamed the Christian Methodist Episcopal Church in 1954). By the onset of the war, separate black congregations existed among all the major denominations, including Presbyterians, Congregationalists, and Episcopalians, but they were few in comparison with the Baptists and Methodists, and none except the latter two groups developed into independent denominations.

The deliberate separation from the white church was the strongest possible statement of the black Christians' rejection of spiritual dependency in general and of the presumption of white racial prerogative in particular, a principle that was to figure prominently in the historic role of the black church in the development of the black subculture in America. The root causes for black abjuration were always the same—the intransigence inherent in the institutionalization of racial differentialism within the very body of Christ, the unwillingness or the inability of the white Christians to address realistically the critical teachings of the faith they claimed to espouse, and the determination of the black membership to be done with pariahism as the most prominent feature of their participation in the Christian fellowship.

The Uses of the Black Church

The black church was first of all the black man's opportunity to worship God in his own way. In the black church there were no special protocols to compromise his dignity or his human worth, and his spiritual destiny was in his own hands. In a very short time, the local black church became the focus of all the important activities that were a part of black life and culture. The church not only solemnized christenings, marriages, and funerals, it also sponsored community uplift, family togetherness, religious and secular festivals, and a variety of social services totally unavailable to blacks elsewhere in the community. It trained its preachers and sent them out to found other churches. It provided the experience for the political participation that marks full responsibility in a democratic society; and it became in time the progenitor of dozens of schools and colleges and academies aimed at making the new black estate in America secure, responsible, and rewarding.

Inside the Black Church

Worship in the black churches varied with the cultural experience of those involved. Those churches whose principal memberships were made up of blacks who had attended the segregated white churches were generally less expressive in worship than those whose experience was shaped in the underground black churches or who had continued the camp meeting traditions of the Great Awakening. The black denominations had adopted wholesale the creedal confessions and the governing and ritual formats of their white counterparts, except for those necessary changes giving recognition to the full sovereignity of black churches and the full humanity and responsibility of black people. Hence, black Christians drew upon four principal traditions: (1) the more formal and less expressive services of the Presbyterians, Episcopalians, Congregationalists, etc.; (2) the less restrained worship of the Baptists and Methodists; (3) the exuberant camp meeting tradition with its extensive lay involvement; and (4) the vestigial African ritual traditions like the "ring dance," which lingered in isolated slave communities such as the Sea Islands of the South Atlantic Coast. All these traditions found their expression in the black church. In consequence, long after the Civil War the ring dance was still a feature of some black churches. Demonstrative preaching, fervent praying, and singing of spirituals were routine. Funerals were extravagant and complex; "shouting," and "testifying" and "talking back" to the preacher were, and in many churches remain, an integral part of the worship service. "Praise houses" still exist in the southeastern United States. On the other hand, worship services in some black churches were, and are, hardly distinguishable from those of the typical white church of the same denomination. Precisely because religion reflects humanity's most significant experiences and values, the genius of the black church as an institution has always been its ready adaptation to the peculiar needs of its people at whatever level or style their spiritual disposition demanded.

The Black Preacher and the Business of Preaching

The black preacher represents one of the most remarkable developments in the history of Christianity in the West. Barred by law and custom from even the rudiments of literacy, shut out from professional associations with other religious leaders who might have lessened somewhat the awesome burden of his ministry by their fellowship and moral support, the black preacher, except for his God, was on his own. To be sure, occasional white pastors befriended individual blacks who felt themselves called to preach, but the established white clergy routinely dismissed such calls as either spurious, or presumptuous, or both. The "business of preaching" was scarcely an undertaking considered appropriate to, or, for that matter, within the capabilities of, black men. The prevailing convention was that the business of preaching was "for mighty few white folks and no niggers a ' tall," and if that dictum did not originate with the established clergy, it did receive from them a very fervent amen! Nevertheless, few blacks who felt themselves under spiritual orders were deterred by popular disapproval. They accepted the ridicule and the risks along with the challenge and the chance to be relevant in the shaping of the Kingdom of God as they understood it. Once the live coal touched their lips, they went forth to prophesy. Pioneer black preachers like Andrew Bryan of Georgia, who preached to whites as well as blacks, were whipped repeatedly in a determined effort to discourage their zeal. Joseph Evans, a free black, risked his freedom and his life when he began preaching in Fayetteville, North Carolina, around 1780, because he found the blacks there "suffering greatly for want of moral and spiritual uplift." Whipped for preaching in Fayetteville, he held clandestine meetings in the outlying sandhills and other remote places. On three occasions he broke the ice of the Cape Fear River to swim to the faithful black Christians who risked being flogged and sold away from their families to hear him preach. His persistence and their faithfulness made history, for the slavemasters became so impressed by the salutary efforts of his preaching that they eventually permitted him to build a small church. Evans's was the first Methodist church in that part of North Carolina, and so many whites eventually came to hear him that the black congregants were crowded out of the sanctuary and separate sheds had to be built for them. When Evans retired in 1808, the grateful white membership had living quarters built for him behind the church, and he occupied those until his death in 1810. A white minister was called to succeed him, and thereafter the church became all white.[11]

Although Evans's remarkable reversal of fortune, including the transition of this church from black to white, was unusual, black preachers who had white or mixed congregations were not altogether rare despite the improbability of such an event. One of the most celebrated preachers of the postrevolutionary era was Harry Hosier, or "Black Harry," a servant and traveling companion to Methodist Bishop Francis Asbury. Black Harry's acclaim as a preacher was so great that, it is said, wherever they journeyed, "people flocked to greet the bishop and to hear Black Harry preach!" His accomplishments are well documented in Bishop Asbury's journal and in other literature of the period. Dr. Benjamin Bush, the famous Philadelphia Quaker and humanitarian, called Harry "the greatest orator in America." Bishop Coke, with whom he traveled in 1784, regarded him as "one of the best preachers in the world . . . even though he cannot read."[12] Harry's acclaim as a preacher seemed in no way diminished by his lack of formal education, a disability common to most black preachers, for what he lacked in literacy, he made up in his uncanny ability to sense and to speak to the peculiar needs of his audiences, whatever their color, and to dramatize the gospel response to those needs. Many black preachers committed large segments of the Bible to memory; some were adept and moved at prayer and in singing. But it was not merely the black preacher's mastery of technique that gave him leadership and power: God was his first credential; conviction his first credibility. He had to be believable in the role in which he cast himself, and he had to be the first to believe.

A very few black preachers were not only literate but learned. North Carolina's John Chavis, a man of "un-mixed African stock," was sent to Princeton by the white Presbyterians of his area to test the widely held theory that Africans were uneducable. After his studies at Princeton and at Washington College as well, Chavis was recognized in 1801 by the General Assembly of the Presbyterian Church as "a black man of prudence and piety" and appointed a missionary to blacks in Virginia and North Carolina.

After five years in the missionary field where he preached frequently to mixed congregations, Chavis opened a private school in Raleigh. To it came the sons of the most prominent white families, and included among its graduates were some of the state's most distinguished public figures.[13]

In New England, Lemuel Haynes, a Congregational minister and a black veteran of the Revolutionary War, pastored white churches and served as a missionary to whites in Vermont, New York, and Connecticut from about 1780 until his death in 1833. Samuel Ringgold Ward, a black Presbyterian preacher in New York, also pastored white churches. Even in the South, black preachers routinely preached to any white who would hear them, and some whites joined their churches despite the inconveniences of slavery. In addition to Joseph Evans and John Chavis, who were free men, George Bently in Tennessee, "Uncle Jack" in Virginia, and "Caesar" in Alabama, all slaves, pastored white or mixed congregations, converting blacks and whites alike. The Alabama Baptist Association purchased Caesar's freedom in 1825 as a gesture of appreciation for his ministry to both blacks and whites. Joseph Willis, a free black from South Carolina, founded the first Baptist church west of the Mississippi in Louisiana in 1805 and four other Baptist churches by 1818. He was highly regarded by the whites among whom he preached, and he was honored as the father of the Baptist church in Louisiana.

The rank and file of black preachers was of course limited to less exotic but no less demanding ministeries in the black churches. Their organizational and political skills were in that context second only to their spiritual gifts in importance. The fledgling black churches they led had no secure financial base and no managerial talent except that developed under the leadership of the black preachers, whose life experience was most often limited to the plantation routine. But they did have spirit, and they did have staying power. Inspired, believing, faithful, Christian men and women working under the humble imprimator of the black church accomplished far more than the souls they saved, the churches they built, the schools they established, the youth they inspired, and the leadership they nourished. They were the true culture builders who in their singular pilgrimage to religious autonomy and spiritual and cultural respectability survived the wastage of slavery, and gave to America a distinctive, alternative religious heritage of which she may well be proud.

Religious Pluralism:
Catholics, Jews, and Sectarians

DAVID EDWIN HARRELL, JR.

On the occasion of this celebration of southern evangelicalism I feel, unjustly no doubt, like a Campbellite in the woodpile. I have been summoned to speak a word about those other southerners; that is, those other white southerners, who, like black southerners, were also religious southerners. That is no simple task. It has not been easy through the years for a Church of Christ boy to find his way through the maze of Holiness and Pentecostal brush arbors into the bejeweled charismatic edifices that grace every modern southern city. But I knew the Pentecostals were there. I had seen their rustic buildings on the dirt streets of south Georgia's villages and some of my poorer kinfolks were given to spiritual ecstasy and heavenly languages. But Catholics and Jews? What in the name of religion do Catholics and Jews have to do with the Fire-Baptized Pentecostal Holiness church? I confess that I can think of one and only one religious attribute shared by southern Catholics, Jews, and sectarians—they are not Baptists or Methodists. Thereon hangs a tale.

The tale has first to do with religious pluralism in the South. Sure enough, it must be admitted that there is religious diversity in the South. In his "Introduction" to *Religion in the Southern States,* Samuel S. Hill struggled heroically to get a dust jacket around West Virginia and Louisiana, Maryland and Oklahoma (not to speak of Florida, he veritably swore) before concluding that, untidy though the picture be, "geographers and students of regional cultures in America do finally depict this sprawl of states

59

and communities as some kind of region, with reference to religion as much as to any single factor." The glue that holds the South together, Hill argued, is an "Anglo-Saxon Protestant hegemony." "The Baptists, the Methodists, and the Presbyterians, usually in that order, are the dominant religious bodies." "Any area where that pattern is disrupted," he concluded, "is referred to as an exception."[1] Among the areas noted as exceptions were Catholic Louisiana and Texas, German Protestant concentrations in Texas, Virginia, and the Carolinas, the "sectarian profusion" in the Appalachian Highlands, Disciples of Christ strength in Kentucky, and the Church of Christ stronghold in middle Tennessee. If post-World War II developments are considered, Hill would be forced to exclude most of Florida, to note the growth of charismatic and Catholic influence in most southern cities (Tulsa is dominated by independent charismatic institutions), and the continued religious diversification of the upper South. Otherwise, at least on the surface, southern religion is homogeneous.

Generally speaking, religious pluralism in the South has been viewed in such denominational blocks. Catholics and Jews existed as religious islands except for a few subregions. Two waves of sectarian division in the nineteenth century left behind pockets of dissenters. In the early nineteenth century, the Disciples of Christ and the Cumberland Presbyterians were successful in some areas of the upper South, in Arkansas, and in Texas, and in the 1890s the Churches of Christ, several Holiness churches, and the Pentecostals spread throughout the South. Virulent and expansive as these religions were in the twentieth century, they still seemed to highlight the Baptist-Methodist hegemony. After all, as John B. Boles reminded in a speech before the Southern Historical Association in 1982, the pie-shaped charts in Edwin Gaustad's religious atlas confirm the dominance of these frontier churches.[2] Although religious counting surely favors record-keeping middle-class churches as opposed to the churches of the poor and although no religious statistics have adequately measured the twentieth-century sectarian growth in the South, the Baptist and Methodist pies will be left for closer examination a bit later.

First, one must speak of those other religious southerners— alienated in an unfriendly evangelical culture. They did sometimes express such feelings. Veteran Church of Christ debater Foy E. Wallace, Jr., wrote in his book *Bulwarks of the Faith:* "The protestant denomination known as the Baptists are the boldest people of the so-called 'orthodox denominations' in pressing their peculiar tenets, and they are perhaps the most flourishing. In some states in the Union they are in control of state and municipal government by influence, and vie with Roman Catholicism in their reach for political power."[3] Perhaps more than any Protestant group, Pentecostals felt alienated and persecuted. They were subjected to a constant barrage of ridicule and verbal abuse and sometimes to violent attacks. And, while anti-Catholicism and anti-Semitism ebbed and flowed in southern history, the potential for such persecution constantly reminded those groups of their minority status.

But it would be nonsense to argue that southern Catholics, Jews, and sectarians were strangers in their native land. In those subregions they dominated, they created societies much like the evangelical South surrounding them. For the most part, they felt perfectly at home with their southern religious neighbors. Fred J. Hood recently wrote of Kentucky's Catholic population: "Surprisingly, much of that is rural Anglo-Saxon; the remainder is centered in the urban areas of Covington and Louisville and made up of the descendants of the German and Irish who migrated to Kentucky before the Civil War. These people blend into the Kentucky cultural landscape with scarcely a discernible difference except for their Catholicism."[4] "In a sense," confirmed Randall Miller in *Catholics in the Old South,* "Catholicism converged with the dominant evangelical Protestantism of the Old South."[5] Recent studies of Jews in such southern cities as Birmingham, Nashville, New Orleans, and Richmond have

confirmed that southern Jews were quintessential southerners—
sometimes passing down family legends of ancestors who participated in the founding of the Ku Klux Klan.[6] "Except for different religious practices," wrote the editors of a recent book on
Jews in the South, "Jews made every effort to become absorbed
into the activities of their adopted home. Their life-style closely
resembled that of their gentile neighbors, and this is one reason
they have failed to attract the attention of historians."[7] In those
periods when a southern civil religion has been most clearly
defined, the Catholics, Jews, and sectarians of the region have
participated in it, contributed to it, and helped to mold it. Their
existence says little more about religious pluralism in the South
than the presence of Presbyterians, Methodists, and Baptists.

On the other hand, southern Catholics, Jews, and sectarians
do call attention to two types of diversity that have existed in the
South, diversity that has meanings reaching far beyond those
groups. Exploring that pluralism will surely be an important
agenda for the next generation of southern religious historians.

First, these groups represent distinctive theological traditions
and, as such, they illustrate the intellectual diversity of the section. Although all religion in the South (as in other regions)
showed a remarkable capacity to bend to social pressure—
accommodating slavery and segregation, lionizing the Lost
Cause, and heralding southern spiritual superiority—each tradition was a repository of unique ideas. The way in which these
belief systems produced culturally distinctive southerners is only
beginning to be explored. Catholicism and Judaism clearly influenced how some southerners viewed marriage, children, education, and drinking. Sectarians were sometimes pacifists, opposed labor organizations, refused to raise tobacco, and, in those
democratic religious societies ruled by the moving of the Holy
Spirit, allowed women to preach and broke racial barriers in
unpredictable ways. In more recent years theological beliefs
have provided bases for conflicting views on abortion, Israel,
creationism, and countless other important questions. In short,
southerners did not and do not believe the same things.

To speak of such religious pluralism in the South also demands acknowledgement that the great evangelical hegemony in the region is a trinity somewhat less united in mind than the Godhead. Are the historical belief systems of these churches irrelevant, in spite of thousands of volumes of theological treatises and doctrinal debate? Is it meaningless that some southerners were Calvinists and others Arminians, some biblical literalists and others pietists? Are there no intellectual reasons for the reunion of northern and southern Methodists in 1939, Presbyterians in 1983, and Baptists at some magic moment after the rapture? The idea of a hegemony suffers particularly when the three mainstream groups are compared with the sects. Intellectually and culturally, many southern Baptists would have identified easily with a Church of Christ throughout southern history (a majority of Landmark Baptist churches were called Baptist Church of Christ) but would have felt thoroughly estranged in a downtown Methodist or Presbyterian church. After all, the Separate Baptists were the first great sectarian group in the South, sounding in Rhys Isaac's sonorous descriptions like a prototype for later southern sects.[8] And, in spite of all that has happened since the descent of Shubal Stearns into North Carolina, Baptists may be the last great sectarian movement in the South as well. Denominational history (properly defined) is still the best avenue to explore the diverse theological traditions in the South.

To suggest that a study of southern sectarianism demands consideration of the major evangelical churches as well as the splinter groups in the region is to inject class tension into the study of southern religion. This pluralism will reveal much about the diversity of southern society and will finally connect the study of southern religion to the region's exploding historiography. For decades southern historians have been exploring clashes between the planter elite and yeoman farmers in the antebellum South; in recent years no subject has enamored southern historians more than the class struggles in the New South at the turn of the twentieth century. C. Vann Woodward's

Origins of the New South, published in 1951, triggered a deluge of books on economic and social history.[9] Although those studies have raised many subtle questions about the nature of the class tensions in the New South, Lacy K. Ford has summed up their general impact in a recent article in the *Journal of American History:* "In the South, as in other areas of the developing world, dramatic economic transformation both created bitter new social conflicts and aggravated long-standing antagonisms."[10] This body of literature has laid bare the complexity of nineteenth-century southern society; it is time to ponder the religious pluralism that accompanied the social and political tensions.

Students of Catholic and Jewish history in the South are well aware of the class tensions within those groups. Because of immigration, those stories are qualitatively discrete, although historians in those streams would do well to relate their stories to southern history as well. Jewish history in the South, as in the remainder of the nation, has primarily to do with the sequential migration of Sephardic Jews followed by German (Ashkenazic) Jews in the early nineteenth century and finally by poor East European Jews in the late nineteenth century. Catholic history in the South is filled with intense internal struggle in the face of ethnic and class tensions. The Catholic community in New Orleans, notes Randall Miller, was "divided by class tensions, Old World jealousies, settlement patterns, length of residence in New Orleans (and America), and ideology."[11]

The history of southern sectarians, however, most clearly parallels the development of class tension in the section. The founding of new sects in the South in the 1830s and at the turn of the twentieth century was symbolic of deep divisions within the evangelical churches. The genuine religious pluralism of the region was established during those eras.

For three decades at the turn of the nineteenth century, Lorenzo Dow was the scourge of Calvinists, Jesuits, and other spokesmen for the Devil in the South and West, and a somewhat erratic friend of Methodism and God. But by 1830 he had become pretty thoroughly disenchanted by the growing sophistication of the Methodists. He wrote: "A preacher being asked in the solitary days of Methodism, during the time of their simplicity; why the *Methodists* did not have 'doctors of divinity' boldly replied, our Divinity is not sick! But now matters are reversed; and the *doctors* are to be found at the helm of affairs, to keep pace with other societies, and be like all the nations round about."[12] Most modern historians agree that Lorenzo knew what he was talking about. "By the 1830s," confirms Anne Loveland, "Baptists and Methodists had gained respectability by virtue of their increasing wealth and higher educational level. . . . To become a Baptist no longer obliged one to 'lose standing or influence in society.'"[13]

The changes in the Baptist and Methodist churches—the two great sects of early southern history—were widely visible by the 1830s. After several decades of rapid growth and expansion, both churches began to solidify their gains and to build more adequate organizations. A generation of new leaders also appeared in each church. Early Baptist and Methodist preachers had been earthy men of the people, who like Peyton Pierce Smith of Franklin County, Georgia, began their ministerial careers with a horse and saddle, "a five dollar watch, and five dollars in money."[14] But by the 1830s southern Baptist leaders were Richard Furman, Richard Fuller, and Jesse Mercer, men who, in the words of Baptist historian Albert Henry Newman, were "better educated and abler than those of the past," men destined to "lead the denomination to still nobler achievements."[15] Among the Methodists were William Capers, Henry Bascom, and Martin Ruter, who, in the words of an early Methodist historian, had attained a "higher intellectual culture," had "the commanding attractions of genius," and were destined to receive "a sort of national rather than denominational recognition."[16]

To some extent, the appearance of a new visible class of respectable planters, town dwellers, and urban ministers in the Baptist and Methodist churches left them open to flanking movements by competitors for the loyalty of the plain people. The gains of the Disciples of Christ and the Cumberland Presbyterians were made partly at the expense of, or at least in competition with, the Baptists and the Methodists. Both groups were orthodox, they drew supporters from the same classes as did the larger evangelical churches, and both showed signs of the same upward mobility as the larger churches. They fed on the growing discontent with the new religious elite that had appeared in the older churches.

But if the Disciples and Cumberland Presbyterian schisms betrayed religious class consciousness in the antebellum South, they were only the most visible tip of that dissatisfaction. The best example of class religious tension in the antebellum South was the Baptist antimission movement, a rebellion of which the Disciples were the most separatist wing. Throughout the South in the 1830s and 1840s, rival Baptist associations mushroomed; the movement, according to Bertram Wyatt-Brown, "exhibited deep-seated class antagonisms."[17] By 1844 there were 900 antimission preachers, 1,622 churches, and at least 68,000 members, mostly in the South. The "effect of the antimission movement," writes a modern Baptist historian, "was devastating."[18] According to Robert Torbet, because of the antimission movement "Baptist missionary societies were dwarfed."[19]

The antimission protest was both southern and lower class. The patronizing "religious dandies" who toured the South with the support of missionary societies were regarded by the older Baptist leaders as both foreign and decadent. Elder Joshua Lawrence of Tar River, North Carolina, protested against the "'tyranny of an unconverted, men-made, money-making . . . factoried' priesthood."[20]

The most visible impact of the antimission movement was the formation of Primitive Baptist associations and the appearance of countless "hard-shell," "Hard-rined," "squared-toed," and "broad-brimmed" independent Baptist churches in the rural South. Strongly predestinarian, the Primitives were an obstinate resistance movement among the poor whites against the condescending leadership of their betters. The two major issues in the divisions—Calvinism and the growth of denominational organizations—represented the intellectual alienation of southern poor whites as well as their isolation from institutional religious power in the antebellum South. In 1848 Baptist historian David Benedict described the deep class antagonisms dividing southern Baptists. "It has been my settled opinion for a long time past, that the cause of missions has had but little to do in this business, so very slender is its hold on the minds of the great mass of our community in most parts of the country, however, they are distinguished. . . . The fact is, that personal altercations, rivalships, and jealousies, and local contests for influence and control have done much to set brethren at variance with each other. The mission question is the ostensible, rather than the real cause of the trouble, in many places. New men and new measures have run faster than the old travelers were accustomed to go, and they have been disturbed at being left behind."[21]

The conservative, sectarian temperament of much of the southern Baptist community was reemphasized in the 1850s with the beginning of Baptist Landmarkism. Long associated with the writing of James R. Graves, editor of the *Tennessee Baptist*, Landmark ideas were present before Graves and outlived his influence.[22] The movement was almost entirely southern and constituted a fervent effort to save Baptist churches from liberalism. Based on an ecclesiology that claimed a historical continuity of Baptist local churches back to biblical times, and, consequently, identified the Baptist church as the Church of Christ, the movement was a reaction both to external sectarian assaults and to the growing influence of sophisticated urban ministers. The Landmarkers reasserted the equalitarian Baptist emphasis on the independence of the local church and restated old antimission prejudices against "priestism" and missionary societies.[23] The vigor of the Landmark movement in the South in the 1850s confirmed that the Southern Baptist Convention, even after shedding the Disciples and Primitives, continued to be a predominately rural and sectarian movement.

In summary, the religious pluralism of the antebellum South was not so much a matter of the evangelical churches versus an exotic sprinkling of Catholics, Jews, and sectarians. It was rather a pluralism based on theological differences and class consciousness and it cut across denominational lines.

The Civil War and Reconstruction blurred the class divisions that had surfaced in the 1830s and 1840s and delayed for a generation further sectarian schisms in southern religion. Charles Wilson has chronicled the remarkable identification of southern Christianity with the Lost Cause.[24] The camaraderie of war, defeat, and the economic suffering of the late nineteenth century had a powerful unifying impact on southern religion. In 1925 Edwin Mims noted that for a generation after the war the churches of the South had been "scarcely touched" by the intellectual and cultural changes revolutionizing the North because the section was "so engrossed . . . in the re-ordering of a broken life."[25] The South remained a hotbed of evangelicalism, much of it strongly sectarian. For a generation after the war, southern white churches were characterized by a real, if temporary, equalitarianism. Katherine Du Pre Lumpkin, a well-bred southern lady and Episcopalian who was reared in genteel deprivation during the difficult years at the turn of the century, remembered that her family always attended the yearly summer revival "at the little Baptist church on a hill about two miles distant from our home." Presided over by a "taciturn, withdrawn man" who was "section boss on the railroad," the little country church was attended by the entire community—rich and poor—"save a few special sinners, and everyone knew why they did not come." "Moreover," concluded Miss Lumpkin, "it was seemly. People would not have understood if we had failed to do so."[26] In the midst of this aberrant postwar social disruption, religious strife virtually disappeared in the South. A student of that Baptist Landmark movement noted that the movement disappeared in the 1860s and

1870s because the whole church was "engulfed in the general impoverishment and paralysis of Southern life and culture."[27]

By 1890 new sectarian rumblings were heard, warning of a new internal crisis in southern religion. The leadership of the southern Baptist and Methodist denominations became increasingly identified with the middle-class aspirations of the New South. As a result, those churches began shedding members to the Holiness and Landmark movements, defections that have increased through the years. The Disciples of Christ and the Cumberland Presbyterians also divided—the Churches of Christ becoming the virulent, sectarian southern wing of the Disciples. By the early twentieth century the South had become the incubator of the fastest growing sects in the nation.

Evidence was everywhere apparent by the 1890s that the Baptists and Methodists of the South were developing a mature new leadership. "One who travels about the South," wrote Edwin Mims, "finds in newspapers, in conversations, in public addresses, evidences that there are circles here and there, institutions of learning, . . . that are as enlightened and as free as any in the country."[28] "Emotional religion is to be expected of the [lower and middler classes] and the whole mass of the negroes," wrote a southern intellectual in 1897, but among the "upper classes" in the traditional churches such excesses were no longer tolerated. "It would be almost as strange," he continued, "to hear a 'fire and brimstone' sermon in a fashionable church in the South as it would be to hear a similar deliverance in New York itself."[29] In the last quarter of the nineteenth century the changes in southern Methodism, in both belief and practice, were rapid and far-reaching. The doctrine of holiness was deemphazied, interest in social Christianity grew, the old rigorous standards of dress and restrictions on amusements were relaxed, and a "more adequately trained ministry" appeared.[30] In 1891 Jeremiah Jeter looked back over his long ministry in the Southern Baptist Convention and summarized the changes he had witnessed. On the positive side Jeter listed a growth in the "construction of good meeting houses," more adequate support of ministers, a "striking improvement in the order of religious assemblies," and a greater emphasis on "practical piety." At the same time, he believed there were changes for the worse. Baptists ministers were more learned and refined in the 1890s, but they were lacking in "unction and pathos." Worship, especially in the "city churches," was more orderly but less fervent; Baptists had become more knowledgeable about "religious subjects generally," but were "less carefully indoctrinated than their fathers."[31]

But this movement of southern Baptists and Methodists to middle-class respectability was by no means uniform or complete. Beneath the increasingly visible layer of moderate leadership in southern churches remained a huge conservative sectarian base. Both the Baptist and Methodist churches remained predominately rural and small town in the early twentieth century. Both were still overwhelmingly churches of the plain people. The 1916 religious census confirmed the relative poverty and rurality of both churches. The Southern Baptist Convention in 1916 reported 92.4 percent of its membership "outside the principal cities" and the Methodists 89.8 percent.[32] Baptist historians have noted that at the turn of the century most Baptist preachers in the South were still "country-bred" and "preferred to live on their farms and preach within reach of their homes rather than attempt to plant churches in the towns and cities."[33]

The continued presence of lower-class prejudices in the Southern Baptist church was evidenced by a resurgence of Landmarkism in the 1880s and 1890s. The revival was so powerful that in the 1880s James R. Graves asserted that fifteen of the sixteen Baptist papers published in the South agreed with his positions.[34] By the 1890s the movement once again challenged more moderate Baptist leaders for control of the convention, though it remained largely "a virile grass-roots, people's movement."[35] In a series of battles in the eighties and nineties, the Landmarkers once again attacked the organized mission work of the Southern Baptist Convention, forced the resignation of Professor William H. Whitsitt from Southern Baptist Seminary because he challenged their ecclesiology, and kept constant pressure on such moderate convention leaders as E. Y. Mullins.[36]

Signaling a growing resentment and insecurity among rural and lower-class Baptists, the Landmark agitation at the turn of the century had two effects. First, the movement once again (as Primitives had earlier) slowed the moderating drift in the church. "In the first half of this century," writes a recent historian, "Landmarkism continued to exert a marked influence, especially in church practice and Baptist isolation."[37] Not until the 1950s, according to another modern historian, did Southern Baptist leadership seriously challenge Landmark doctrines.[38] Although the Landmarkers did not control the church's institutions, they powerfully influenced them. They won some important battles, particularly the Whitsitt controversy; all except the most disgruntled believed that their church was not beyond rescue.[39] Most poor and rural Baptists still felt at home in the Southern Baptist Convention in 1920, secure in their independence and isolation, suspicious of the professors in Louisville and the leaders of the city churches, but heartened by periodic assurances of Baptist orthodoxy and a common commitment to evangelization.

A minority of the Landmarkers decided at the turn of the century that they could no longer tolerate the encroachments of liberalism in the church. Led by Ben M. Bogard of Arkansas, nearly 1,500 Baptist churches in the Southwest bolted the Southern Baptist Convention in 1905 and formed a new movement, which came to be called the American Baptist Association. Bogard's paper, *The Baptist and Commoner,* printed in Little Rock, was powerful in the historic "Landmark belt," and by 1926 the Association numbered 117,858 members. In Arkansas it captured 39.4 percent of the Baptist churches in the state, including 41.2 percent of the rural churches.[40]

Parallel to Landmarkism among the Baptists was the Holiness movement in Methodism. The Holiness associations that blossomed in the late nineteenth century served as safety valves for

poor and rural Methodists who were increasingly isolated from
the sources of power within their denomination. The early roots
of the Holiness movement were in the North; the National Association for the Promotion of Holiness was established in 1867 in
New Jersey, after the North had been swept by waves of Holiness
revivalism just prior to the Civil War.[41] As Holiness associations
and campgrounds proliferated in the 1870s and 1880s, northern
Methodist leaders increasingly resisted the movement. A pro-
fane observer wrote: "As the Methodists grew in worldly wealth
and wisdom, the suspicion dawned among their sophisticates that
orgies which notoriously led to female and lay exhortation,
trances and holy turmoil at the altar, were tending to discredit all
socially aspiring members of their denomination with their Episcopalian acquaintances and bankers. Consequently in the last
three decades of the century, their bishops launched a subtle but
determined campaign to put the Holiness movement under re-
straint."[42] The result of such pressure was a growth of "come-
outism" in the northern Holiness movement and the formation of
a number of new sects—the Church of the Nazarene, the Christian and Missionary Alliance, and the Church of God (Anderson,
Indiana) being the most important. These new churches were all
moderate within the Holiness context; they were predominantly
urban (providing way-stations in the cities for the rural Methodists moving into lower-middle-class jobs) and were not particularly strong in the South. In 1916 the largest of the Holiness
bodies, the Church of the Nazarene, reported less than 15 percent of its membership in former Confederate states.[43]

The southern Methodist experience, like the Baptist, was influenced by the cultural solidarity of the South after the Civil War
and the continued prominence of conservative rural influences
within the church. In the 1870s southern Methodist bishops encouraged the Holiness movement, calling for "a general and powerful revival of Scriptural holiness."[44] At the heart of the Holiness
crusade in the 1870s and 1880s in the South were local Methodist
ministers. Vinson Synan reports that in the 1880s "200 of the 240

ministers of the North Georgia Conference professed to have received the experience of sanctification as a 'second blessing' "[45] But in the 1890s southern Methodist leaders moved to quell the growing movement, fearing its potential to encourage doctrinal extremism and separation. Led by Bishop Atticus Haygood, in 1894 the bishops condemned the movement and moved to control its most outspoken promoters.

In short, the Holiness-southern Methodist experience roughly paralleled the Landmark-southern Baptist experience. In each case the conservative movements won wide support among the poor and farmers and retarded the growth of liberalism. "The Methodist preachers are the preservers of every old idea," wrote a disgruntled Methodist at the turn of the century, "timid to the point of cowardice."[46] In the South a large number of the Holiness campgrounds continued to operate under Methodist control. At the same time, the Holiness splinters in the South tended to attract only the most radical and doctrinally extreme Methodist. Although the moderate Holiness churches did grow in the South in the 1890s, establishing colleges in four states, the southern "come-outers" were strongly influenced by B. H. Irwin's "fire-baptized" movement, which urged the sanctified to press on to additional baptisms—including "dynamite, lyddite, and oxydite."[47] The small, exclusively southern, splinter Holiness sects, which began to appear in the census by 1916, were strikingly poor and rural.[46]

If the two historic southern churches of the plain people were in class tension at the turn of the century, clear class divisions took place in the two other people's churches, the Disciples of Christ and the Cumberland Presbyterians. Both churches suffered major divisions officially dated in 1906. Both divisions were partly sectional. A small majority of the Cumberland Presbyterians voted to unite with the Presbyterian Church of the United States of America after that body diluted its Calvinistic creed in 1903, but a majority of the southern churches refused to accept the union agreement. At the same time, a majority of the southern Disciples of Christ separated themselves in the 1906 religious census into the Churches of Christ. Theological issues aside, both divisions were sectional and economic. In the case of the Cumberland Presbyterians, sectional prejudices and race fears played a part in the rejection of the merger by many southern churches. The 1916 census reveals that the uniting churches were also larger and wealthier. Although just over 50 percent of the Cumberland Presbyterian churches joined the northern church, they carried with them two-thirds of the value of church buildings and over three-quarters of the value of parsonages in the denomination. The churches that remained Cumberland Presbyterian had contributed less than 20 percent of the church's domestic missions budget in 1906. One promerger leader charged that his opponents were "anti-church-erection, anti-mission, anti-education and anti-everything."[49] After the merger, the Cumberland Presbyterian church became even more rural than before; in 1916 less than 5 percent of its membership attended churches in towns of over 25,000 population.[50] The church also remained poor. Only about one-fourth of its ministers in 1916 were seminary graduates and about 40 percent were farmers. Those reporting to the census as "full-time pastors" earned annual wages of $607.[51]

Even clearer is the sectional and urban-rural character of the division in the Disciples of Christ.[52] In 1916 the Church of Christ (the name taken by the conservative wing of the movement) claimed 196,835 members in the former states of the Confederacy (61.9 percent of its total membership) as opposed to 185,144 for the Disciples of Christ in the same states (15.1 percent of its national membership). The schism followed clear class lines as well as sectional. The Church of Christ outnumbered the Disciples in the mid-South and Southwest while it was outnumbered in the coastal states and in the cities everywhere. In Memphis each group had four churches but the Disciples led in membership 1,688 to 368; in Birmingham there were two Churches of Christ with 250 members and three Disciples of Christ congregations with 645 members; in Little Rock there was one Church of Christ with sixty-five members and three Disciples of Christ churches with 1,139 members; in Dallas the eight Churches of Christ had 997 members and eleven Disciples churches had 3,122. In southern towns with populations of over 25,000 in 1916 only Nashville, the center of Church of Christ influence, reported more Churches of Christ than Disciples.[53] The Church of Christ was the most rural major religious group listed in the census of 1916, reporting 95.5 percent of its membership "outside of principal cities."[54]

The economic statistics collected by the census confirmed this pattern. The average value of church edifices reported by the Church of Christ in 1916 was $1,101.30; for the Disciples of Christ it was $4,803.14. In Alabama the figures were: Disciples of Christ $3,188.14, Churches of Christ $863.65; in Arkansas: Disciples of Christ $2,363.00, Churches of Christ $606.98. The average value of a Disciple church in the south was $3,516.73, that of a Church of Christ $962.32. The average membership of a Disciples congregation was 146; that of a Church of Christ fifty-seven.[55] Nor were the crusty farmer-preachers who led the Church of Christ division unaware of what was happening. In 1897 one editor explained the schism: "As time advanced such of those churches as assembled in large towns and cities gradually became proud, or, at least, sufficiently worldly-minded to desire popularity, and in order to attain that unscriptural end they adopted certain popular arrangements such as the hired pastor, the church choir, instrumental music, man-made societies to advance the gospel and human devices to raise money to support previously mentioned devices of similar origin. In so doing they divided the brotherhood of disciples."[56]

For the most part, this religious turmoil had to do with the resentments of small farmers, and, particularly in the case of the Holiness movement, small-town artisans and laborers. A nineteenth-century Church of Christ preacher described his church as the "industrious, sober and comparatively moral

poor."[57] But by the 1920s another white social class had emerged
in the South. Writing in 1925, Edwin Mims reported that the
South had an educated elite who were much like their peers in
the North, another class of "half-educated, who have very little
intellectual curiosity or independence of judgement" (a group
that might well include the morally upright Landmarkers, the
Church of Christ, the Holiness, Cumberland Presbyterians, and
Primitives), and a third class composed of "a great mass of un-
educated people—sensitive, passionate, prejudiced."[58] Among
this group, the abjectly poor, the tenants, and the mill workers,
Pentecostalism flourished in the early twentieth century. By the
1920s the South had become, and for a generation remained, the
nation's best neighborhood in which to peddle the gospel of poverty. This teeming layer of southern religion seldom came into
public view; rural southern Methodists and Baptists were curious
enough to baffle most urban Americans in the 1920s. H. L.
Mencken, at the peak of his career of ridiculing Baptists,
Methodists, and southerners, was utterly stunned to witness
brother Joe Furdew preaching to an outdoor "holy roller" meeting in the hills near Dayton during the Scopes trial. As he returned from the meeting late in the evening, Mencken surveyed
the scene in Dayton: "There was the friar wearing a sandwich
sign announcing that he was the Bible Champion of the world.
There was a Seventh Day Adventist arguing that Clarence Dar-
row was the beast with seven heads and ten horns described in
Revelation XIII, and that the end of the world was at hand. There
was an evangelist made up like Andy Gump, with the news that
atheists in Cincinnati were preparing to descend upon Dayton,
hang the eminent Judge Raulston, and burn the town. There was
the eloquent Dr. T. T. Martin, of Blue Mountain, Miss., come to
town with a truck-load of torches and hymn-books to put Darwin
in his place." But as the crowd dispersed to Robinson's Drug
Store for a Coke, Mencken mused that the air of true "devotion"
was missing. "The real religion was not present," he wrote. "It
began at the bridge over the town creek, where the road makes

off for the hills."[59] What Mencken had learned was that Dayton was to Rhea County what Atlanta was to Georgia and Paris to France. If the God-fearing people of Dayton, southern sectarians all, were an embarrassment to urban southern Baptists and Methodists, they seemed shamelessly decadent to the Pentecostals in the hills.

By 1920 the three largest Pentecostal churches in the South were the Assemblies of God, with headquarters in Springfield, Missouri; the Pentecostal Holiness church, headquartered in Franklin Springs, Georgia; and the Church of God, with headquarters in Cleveland, Tennessee. All three of the churches had direct connections to the Holiness movement. When the Pentecostal experience of speaking in tongues rushed through the American holiness movement after the Azusa Street meeting in Los Angeles in 1906, it found its readiest reception in the South. As southern Pentecostalism developed in the early twentieth century it tended to be more radical doctrinally, less interested in cooperation with the organized Fundamentalist movement, and more rural than its northern counterpart.[60] The first major split in the movement involved the question of whether the baptism of the Holy Spirit was the second or third work of grace, and a majority of southern Pentecostals (the Pentecostal Holiness church and the Church of God) took the more radical third-work view. This doctrinal stance clearly indicated the influence of Methodism in southern Pentecostalism.[61] Although there was a sprinkling of Baptists among early southern Pentecostals, and some minor Baptist groups—particularly the Free Will Baptists—became wholehearted participants in the Pentecostal revival, generally poor Baptists felt more at home in their churches than did poor Methodists by the turn of the century.[62] At least, southern Methodism was less able or willing to accommodate radicalism and independence than the Southern Baptist church.

The theological roots of southern Pentecostalism are somewhat diverse, but the movement was uniformly successful among the lower class. In 1916 the Assemblies of God reported 118 congregations, including forty-seven in the South. Only thirty of the southern churches owned church buildings; they averaged $734.26 in value. This small denomination of 6,703 members reported 600 ministers, a ratio of one minister to eleven members. Only twenty-seven of these ministers received salaries; the average was $578 per year.[63] The Church of God reported 202 congregations and 7,784 members, almost all in the South. The average value of a church building in the sect was $586.26. The Church of God claimed 477 ministers and eighty-one reported wages averaging $232 per year.[64]

By 1920 a bewildering array of Pentecostal sects was competing in the South, reflecting endless nuances in their hostility to the alien culture around them. Most were rigidly puritanical; the "frivolities" of the rich were condemned, including "moving picture shows, baseball games, picnics, circuses, dancing halls, county and state fairs," and other activities "calculated to destroy spirituality." Members were required to avoid "oath-bound secret societies, social clubs, and corrupt partisan politics."[65] In 1928 a bewildered outsider caricatured Pentecostal beliefs: "In all their sects the Holy Rollers are against the vices of infidelity, evolutionism, sexual recreation, the use of gin, and fallen Methodism. They are against plain prayer without orgies as much as they are against dancing, liquor and tobacco. They are against faith without a personal Devil as much as they are against jewelry, tea and coffee, transparent female garments, polygamy and theological liberalism."[66]

There were significant variations within this religious fringe. The moderate Church of the Nazarene attributed speaking in tongues to the "power of the devil" and in 1919 removed the word "Pentecostal" from its name "to dissassociate themselves from what seemed to them fanaticism."[67] At the same time, many Pentecostals were disgusted by the Nazarene emphasis on education, despite one Nazarene college adopting as its school yell,

"Hallelujah." But even the more rigid Pentecostal churches were plagued by divisions because of small accommodations to the world. In the 1930s the Pentecostal Holiness church relaxed an earlier law and allowed its members to belong to labor unions "consistent . . . with the legal effort on the part of labor, to prevent oppression and injustice from capitalism."[68] Members were required not to use, sell, or grow tobacco, but in a concession to the poor of the tobacco farming belt, the church's *Discipline* added exceptions in the 1930s: "The word 'growth' in regard to tobacco shall not apply to hired help, or wives, and children who are required to work for tenants or landlords."[69] As early as 1917 the Pentecostal Holiness church established standards for ordination that required a candidate to "recite in consecutive order the Books of the Bible," to "read the Bible through twice, and in addition to read at least 1,000 pages of other suggested books in harmony with the doctrines of the Pentecostal Holiness Church."[70] The Church of God was criticized by other Pentecostals when in the mid-1920s it allowed its members to wear "wedding rings costing less than five dollars . . . in communities where their absence would cause scandal."[71] On the fringe, the Church of God with Signs Following, founded in 1909, scorned all other Pentecostals who refused to handle serpents.[72]

In summary, the decade of the 1890s was a watershed in southern religious history as well as in southern political history. Most visible was the growing identification of the old churches of the people with the new southern elite. "Southern white Protestantism," wrote historian Frederick Bode, "(unwittingly or not) became one of the mechanisms of the ruling-class hegemony."[73] The point, however, is not so much whether the Baptists and Methodists either wittingly or unwittingly were captured (or bribed) by the business elite to legitimate the New South, but that the leaders in those churches increasingly came to believe in the vision themselves. They were a part of the new elite. "Religion," wrote Methodist Bishop Raymond Brown of Arkansas, "grabbed hold of the coat-tails of secular prosperity and growth."[74]

As always, the upward mobility of the old churches of the plain people was only part of the story. Though not directly related to Populism, the sectarian religious revolt at the turn of the century was clearly a parallel movement. The new southern middle class captured only one segment of southern evangelicalism. Many southern churches continued to be dominated by sturdy and moral small farmers and laborers. For some southerners the religious crisis meant a continued but increasingly loose connection with their old churches, but for others conscience demanded secession. This religious class consciousness turned the South into a caldron of sectarianism for half a century. The South, which had endured for three quarters of a century without the introduction of a significant new religious group and in which the old popular churches had seemed to be classless, suddenly became a maze of class consciousness in which Liston Pope found Presbyterians looking down on Baptists and Methodists who regarded the Church of God as a group of fanatics.[75] And, in fact, on closer inspection, one can find Baptists looking down on Baptists, Catholics on Catholics, and Jews on Jews.

In summary, southern religion has been molded by the distinctive history of the region; Catholics, Jews, and sectarians have shared in that experience. But the religious history of the section is also rich and diversified. The distinctions were often subtle, difficult to explain to outside canvassers. In 1940 the pastor of the Central Christian Church in Fayetteville, Arkansas, tried to explain to the Historical Records Survey office in Little Rock the nuances within her religious movement: "I can understand your perplexity as to how Central Christian Church should be classified. We hardly know how to tell you. . . . In the course of a century and a half, a rather complete denominational setup has developed, repudiated by the great middle-class rank and file, but fostered by a very skillfull minority which controlled the conventions and gave out misleading publicity to the press. It by no means represents the principles underlying the move-ment. . . . The lines I have indicated are not sharply defined. Many churches whose names appear in the Disciples of Christ yearbook have their fingers crossed about the whole setup, and believe in local autonomy, just as we do. Often both groups are represented in the same congregation. It is an unsatisfactory situation, but desire for unity has prevented a clear-cut break, in the large. I wish you could devise a method of classification which would more truly represent the situation."[76] The survey completed by the WPA at the close of the Depression is filled with such feelings of ambivalence. For instance, a worker tried to describe the Friendship Missionary Baptist Church, which met in Amos school house in Baxter County, Arkansas: "Mr. M. L. Crownover's mother helped organize the church and was assisted by Rev. Jennings, the first pastor. But the church has changed in some respects. The pastor is considered a Landmarker. . . . Some of the old members of the Missionary Baptist Church there still have their membership in the Church. But the pastor is strictly Landmarker. However the church is a Missionary Baptist."[77] And there was the Beebe and Arkansas Camp Meeting Association, established in 1894 by a "Holiness Band" of Methodists aided by a sprinkling of Baptists. The 1941 historical survey recorded the campground's religious pilgrimage: "Denominations which have furnished preachers are Methodist, Quakers, Pilgrims, Baptist, Christians, Presbyterians and Nazarines [sic]. For the past few years there has been more Nazarine preachers than from the other denominations. I was told the reason was, that the preacher has to preach holiness and it was easier to get a preacher from the Nazarine than other denominations."[78]

At the close of the recent book on Catholics in the Old South, which he edited with Randall Miller, Jon L. Wakelyn listed the kinds of questions the volume intended to raise: "The key issues continue to be those of what it meant to be Catholic, Southern and to live in the South. How Catholics who lived in the South

held on to their faith and the extent to which their faith influenced their various activities is essential to understanding how
they lived in the South. How they identified as Catholic and the
dissension among various Catholics, too, reveal their relationship
to Southern society."[79] Historians need to ask these same questions about all religious southerners. What has it meant to be a
Pentecostal, or an Orthodox Jew, or a Campbellite, or a Landmark Baptist and a southerner as well? And what have the internal tensions within southern religion had to do with the general
history of the region. Only when these questions have been addressed will southern religious historiography approach in
sophistication the recent writing about the region's social, economic, and political history.

"Feeding the Hungry and Ministering to the Broken Hearted":

The Presbyterian Church in the United States and the Social Gospel, 1900–1920

J. WAYNE FLYNT

As the Reverend Walter L. Lingle, pastor of Atlanta's First Presbyterian Church, browsed among magazines in that city's Carnegie Library in 1909, he happened upon an article by Ray Stannard Baker. The essay that attracted his attention dealt with Christianity and the nation's social problems. He read quickly through the article and noted Baker's enthusiastic reference to a new book by Baptist theologian Walter Rauschenbusch entitled *Christianity and the Social Crisis.* Lingle moved through the stacks until he located the book, then read it with deepening interest. On the twentieth anniversary of that first discovery, Lingle delivered the James Sprunt Lectures at Union Theological Seminary in Richmond, Virginia. He chose for his subject the "Social Teachings of the Bible." Remembering his first reading of Rauschenbusch, he wrote: "It is a dynamic work. Since that time, I have read many volumes on the same general subject, but no other book has so stirred my soul as that first one."[1]

By the time the General Assembly of the Presbyterian Church in the United States (the southern branch of Presbyterianism) met in May, 1911, Rauschenbusch's influence had spread. The

Committee on Theological Seminaries, "in view of the growing importance of many social questions," recommended that all PCUS Seminaries "adopt and teach a brief, practical course in Sociology." The recommendation was adopted, and within the month A. L. Phillips, the general superintendent of the Committee of Publication, wrote Lingle confidentially testing his reaction to becoming a professor at Union Seminary in Richmond. The most distinguished PCUS seminary wanted a professor to teach practical theology including subjects such as modern Sunday School, young people's societies, missions, church finance and other issues involving a minister's adjustment to life in a modern society. Phillips had heard that Lingle advocated such changes "with great force and conviction" from the pulpit of Atlanta's First Presbyterian Church, which he pastored. His duties would also include teaching a new course on Christianity and the social order, a subject of growing interest to Lingle. So the times and the man met. Lingle resigned his pastorate and moved his family to Richmond where he began a new and influential ministry interpreting and advocating the Social Gospel.[2]

For many years historians simply ignored the Walter Lingles of the South. Treating the Mason-Dixon Line as an impenetrable barrier to reform, they discussed Populism, Progressivism, the labor movement, and the Social Gospel as if such movements had never occurred in the South. With the discovery of a persistent reform tradition dating to the earliest years of the region, this notion has now been considerably modified. Recently intellectuals have even conceded that the South produced a highly developed culture, a notion that no doubt would have H. L. Mencken rejoicing in paradise, had he believed in paradise. Historians of southern religion have discovered numerous nineteenth-century urban pastors well educated in the theological ideas current in Europe, a rich and meaningful tradition of folk religion, and even a Social Gospel.

The Social Gospel is a concept generally applied to a specific period of American religious history, beginning in the late nineteenth century, flourishing between 1900 and 1920, then slowly declining, though not without bursts of renewed vigor. Recent historians argue that the Social Gospel was not primarily a set of theological ideas, a new kind of Christianity, or a uniform movement. Experiences were more influential than ideas, especially those of urban pastors with the poor and with immigrants. Social Gospelers discussed theological ideas but filled their writings, lectures, and sermons with calls for action. Their primary concern was the city, which became a mission field for the conversion and Americanization of immigrants and the expression of Christian concern for the poor. The Social Gospel movement occurred in the context of change, excitement, and hope for a more just society. Although its critics viewed Social Christianity as an aberrant, new form of Christianity, its advocates stressed their allegiance to traditional Christian concepts such as sin, conversion, salvation, regeneration, holiness, repentance, perfection, and the Kingdom of God. They merely attempted to apply such ideas to society rather than exclusively to individuals.[3]

Within the Social Gospel movement diverse elements competed for influence. The largest group was a conservative assortment of pastors, academics, and laypeople who sought evolutionary change. They viewed the future with confidence in the emergence of a just social order. They were cautious and preferred the term "social service" to Social Gospel. They were suspicious of socialism, viewed the church as a mediating force between powerful special interests, and believed that efforts to remake society without converting individuals were doomed to failure. The reforms they advocated such as settlement houses and institutional churches were done *for* the working class, blacks, and the poor. Shailer Mathews, professor of New Testament at the University of Chicago, was one of their leaders.[4]

A smaller, revolutionary Social Gospel faction was more pessimistic about the future of a country dominated by unregulated capitalism. But if Christianity could change the structure of society, social salvation might still be possible. The key, however, was to change structures, not individuals. These social activists worked for more drastic change, often endorsed socialism, and worked *with* the lower classes, believing that the church must take sides on social issues affecting the poor. Walter Rauschenbusch, professor of church history at Rochester Theological Seminary, was the primary spokesman for this viewpoint.[5]

The Social Gospel affected every mainline American religious group. Some it dominated, others it influenced but never controlled, still others it touched only slightly. That it influenced the North more than the South is entirely understandable. There the problems of cities, immigrants, and urban class conflict, precisely the problems most frequently addressed by the Social Gospel, were pronounced. In the South, individualism, the predominance of a rural way of life, and the relatively modest size and complexity of cities presented fewer crises.

Nonetheless it is surprising that historians long ignored the primary sources of the Social Gospel in the South. Happily, the debate no longer revolves around whether the Social Gospel reached the South.[6] Rather the questions concern the extent of the Social Gospel's penetration, the relationship between ideas and action, the determination to redeem social structures rather than just to perform charitable good works, and the extent of its influence within southern denominations.[7]

To put the debate into context, several generalizations are important. First, the South's rural distinctiveness must be understood. Obviously a region with few cities would produce religious concerns somewhat different from a region with many cities. Secondly, the Social Gospel by no means swept the North and Midwest into a consensus on the role of religion and society. The resurgent Fundamentalism of the 1920s demonstrated the continuing diversity quite well. Thirdly, even northern advocates of the Social Gospel acted from mixed motives, which often make it difficult to trace precisely the route from ideas to actions. A recent dissertation on the settlement house movement in Indiana notes that this quintessential Social Gospel reform was initiated not by radicals or socialists nor from a well formed social philosophy. The ideas of settlement house social workers could best be called Christian humanitarianism, which defined sin as social maladjustment. They were not cultural pluralists, but "missionaries for the American way." They desired to convert Catholic immigrants not only to Protestantism but into proper Americans like themselves. Protestant settlement workers in Indiana generally attributed poverty to "a failure of will or character deficiency in the victim," not to structural problems within capitalism.[8] If in order to validate the Social Gospel, the relationship of ideas to action must be precise, the concern for redeeming social structures paramount, the extent of Social Gospel penetration pronounced, perhaps the Social Gospel did not exist in Indiana or the South.

The issue is too significant to hinge on a debate over semantics. Because so many of the South's liberals traced their roots to religious forms and ideas, it is tempting to treat this subject biographically. Candidates for such an approach are numerous: Edgar Gardner Murphy, Lucy Randolph Mason, Will Campbell, Aubrey Williams, Will Alexander, Jimmy Carter. Virtually every recent historian who has tackled the South's twentieth-century liberal tradition has commented on the formative and unusually extensive role religion played.[9]

A more formidable and obscure challenge swirls around that solitary 1909 patron of the Carnegie Library in Atlanta. One is not so surprised to find numerous southern Methodist settlement houses for Methodists had prophesied a similar radical message in nineteenth-century England. And the anarchy of Southern Baptists always allows a heretic or two to slip under the ecclesiastical tent on the assumption that the only difference between orthodoxy and heterodoxy is my-doxy and your-doxy. But no more hostile environment could be found for the Social Gospel than the Presbyterian Church in the United States. The church, often viewed as the right wing of the Protestant Reformation, was theocratic, nationalistic, conservative, rationalistic, and sufficiently hierarchial and dogmatic to expel its worst malcontents.[10] If one can find in the PCUS a connection between theological ideas and social action, a fundamental critique of social structures, or influential linkage to mainstream Social Gospel organizations, leaders, and ideas, such discovery should lift the debate to another level.

Ernest Trice Thompson found no such phenomenon. In his splendid three volume history of the denomination, he chronicled substantial social change between 1880 and 1920 but minimized the role of the Social Gospel. As did many others before him, he confined his research to denominational newspapers and official proceedings of presbyteries, synods, and the General Assembly. Although he mentions Walter Lingle and other Social Gospel leaders casually, he did not use their papers. Had he done so, what a treasure would have greeted him.[11]

The barriers to the Social Gospel that the PCUS erected were formidable. In addition to a religious hierarchy, which was, however, much more democratic and tolerant in practice than in theory, there were the individualistic, middle-class, and conservative economic and political values of most Presbyterians.

Like Southern Baptists and Methodists, Presbyterians rejected the new "higher criticism," which was long thought to be a concomitant of the Social Gospel. As best they could they sought to exorcise it from their body. After Lingle arrived in Richmond to teach at Union Seminary he received letters leaving no doubt about the theological views of his friends. A student wrote for suggested theological reading: "I am a pretty strict Presbyterian of several generations back, but I have studied a good deal, and am not afraid of criticism, higher or lower; it can't hurt the Bible." A friend from Atlanta wrote Lingle about possible union of the northern and southern wings of Presbyterianism. He noted in his letter that a northern friend in the PCUSA desired unity also, "as soon as they could weed out about 20% of their cranks and heretics. This old brother knew what he was talking about, didn't he?"[12] Nor did Lingle stray far from biblical orthodoxy.

Some Presbyterians arduously desired to protect parishioners' minds from the poisonous wells of heresy. The secretary-treasurer of the Committee of Publication feared attempts to bring before the 1911 General Assembly a plan to require a censor. The committee had never practiced strict censorship because "Presbyterians have a way of doing their own thinking." But there was "a large element of conservative men scattered over the church who do not seem to understand the difficulties of our position." The issue arose again when the 1912 Assembly dispatched a pastoral letter condemning the International Graded Sunday School Lessons for disseminating "the theories of the school of radical criticism," deemphasis on redemption and the Holy Spirit, and inclusion of too much nonbiblical material. A resolution introduced at the 1920 General Assembly urged the Committee of Publication not to recommend or sell any publications that were "not in full accord with the fundamental belief of our Evangelistic Churches." A substitute softened the resolution only slightly by urging the committee to exercise "scrupulous care" concerning books recommended to Presbyterians.[13] Liberals occasionally rippled the theological waters but not enough to trouble Zion.

Although Presbyterians shared opposition to "higher criticism" with Baptists and Methodists, they were distinctive in their doctrine of the spirituality of the church. Dating back to the origins of the PCUS, the doctrine was partly rooted in New School-Old School theological debates and partly in the pre-Civil War struggle over slavery. A minority of northern Presbyterians condemned slavery and sought to use the church as a forum for abolitionist and pro-Union theory. As part of their rationalization of slavery, southern Presbyterians insisted that the church should not engage in secular politics. It had a legitimate prophetic role to stir the hearts of men who in turn should exercise their rights as citizens. But the institutional church was a spiritual not a social entity and must not soil itself with issues that would inevitably divide its fellowship and compromise its purity.[14]

Even conservative Presbyterians sometimes rankled under this doctrine especially when the issue was demon rum. In 1907 a number of presbyteries from the Synod of Alabama petitioned the General Assembly to appoint a permanent committee on temperance. The Assembly declined replying that the position of the PCUS was well known already and such a measure "would involve the possibility of political entanglements." Not to be denied, the Presbytery of North Alabama in October, 1909, endorsed statewide prohibition, which it called a nonpartisan and nonpolitical moral issue. Dissenters within the presbytery challenged the resolution as a violation of the Book of Church Order, paragraph 248, which established the principle of nonintrusion into civil affairs, but the prohibitionist faction won 14 to 7. By 1915 the issue had spread throughout the denomination. When the General Assembly congratulated the Womens Christian Temperance Union and advised Presbyterians to support a constitutional amendment prohibiting the sale of alcoholic beverages, the Synod of Virginia vigorously opposed the action. Its delegates resolved that attempts to instruct citizens how to vote contravened the principles of the PCUS on the relationship of church to civil government.[15]

Within the denomination the desire to control alcohol abuse clashed with the doctrine of the spirituality of the church, but Walter Lingle decided his position early in the conflict. When a pastor in south Georgia near the turn of the century, his presbytery had turned out an elder who owned a distillery. Prohibiting liquor was the proper business of a Presbyterian as was the "need to carry Christianity into every department of life," Lingle assured a friend. He associated more active social Christianity not with radical departures from historic doctrine, but as a return to the teachings of Christ.[16]

Other moral questions called for the involvement of the church as well, none more so than child labor. D. P. McGeachy had been present when the Synod of Virginia debated the prohibition question in 1915 and had argued that in some cases the church should take a stand on questions involving politics. The debate became so heated that "for the sake of the peace of the house," discussion had been ended. The exchange had persuaded him to prepare a paper for the County Ministers Association on the subject "The Pastor and Social Service." He had read Rauschenbusch, Shailer Mathews, and Presbyterian James Howerton's book, *The Church and Social Reforms*, but remained confused. He asked Lingle to explain precisely what the Bible taught about social service. Although he wrote conservatives for their opinions also and planned to avoid either extreme position, he had already decided to plead for "preaching Christ" in "sermons on prohibition and child slavery [labor]." Was it not "pure cowardice" for Presbyterians to "never open our mouths over any question that might be in any degree political no matter how tremendous the moral issues are that are involved? I take the position that you have to answer questions like that with an 'It depends.'" Every situation had to be confronted as it appeared "keeping to the general principles of the spirituality of the Church. . . ."[17]

Alexander McKelway experienced no such ambivalence. After completing his education at Hampden-Sydney College and Union Theological Seminary, he held pastorates in Virginia and North Carolina until 1898 when he became editor of the most influential PCUS state newspaper, the *Presbyterian Standard*, published in Charlotte, North Carolina. Although McKelway shared the racial ideology of his times, he differed markedly from conservative Presbyterians on the issue of social service. His special concern was the elimination of child labor, but he became involved in a multitude of social causes. As southern director of the National Child Labor Committee, McKelway urged Presbyterian ministers to use their influence for passage of federal legislation limiting child labor. To those who complained that this compromised the purity of Presbyterianism, he responded that "the church loses her hold on the conscience of men when she shrinks from uttering her voice for a righteous cause for fear of political entanglements."[18] A brilliant, acerbic propagandist and

organizer, McKelway played a major role in the creation of the
Southern Sociological Congress, was elected its first vice-
president, and used it effectively in his crusade against child
labor. When President Woodrow Wilson hesitated to adopt the
cause, McKelway bombarded him with propaganda until he
finally capitulated in 1916. In that election year McKelway cam-
paigned devotedly for Wilson and persuaded the Democratic
party to adopt twenty reform proposals for its platform, including
the eight-hour day, a pension system, development of human
welfare agencies, a national child labor law, and prison reform.
After the Democrats accepted nearly all his proposals, he conducted a vigorous effort to win the vote of social workers and
progressives from Theodore Roosevelt's 1912 Progressive party.[19]
Thanks to McKelway's spirited advocacy of child labor, the PCUS
compromised its rigid adherence to the spirituality of the church.
In 1908 the Reverend Dr. R. F. Campbell proposed a strong
resolution to the General Assembly arguing that the legacy of
child labor was "the disintegration of the family, the promotion of
illiteracy, the destruction of church influences. . . ." The resolution urged employers and parents to obey laws already passed
and to strive for more effective legislation. The resolution passed
easily.[20] So effective was McKelway's lobbying and mobilization
of southern churches that by 1910 all southern states had enacted
minimum age laws. McKelway had found a way to translate Social Gospel ideas into legislative reality.

If McKelway's spirited campaign to save the children was the
most serious early breach in the practice of the spirituality of the
church, Dr. James R. Howerton's book was one of the earliest
ideological challenges to that doctrine. Howerton was a professor
of philosophy at Washington and Lee University and an influential Presbyterian minister. In 1909 he began delivering lectures
on the church and social issues. In the mid teens he combined
three lectures into a book entitled *The Church and Social Reforms.* Howerton unsuccessfully tried to harmonize the conflict
between the Social Gospel and the spirituality of the church. In

his third lecture/essay, entitled "The Church and the Social Reforms of Today," he argued that both church and state sought the same end, the moral welfare of humanity. But the church must communicate a message of social salvation to its members, not act coercively or engage in secular reforms as an institution. The church must reform law by reforming lawyers, politics by reforming politicans, society by reforming social leaders. But she could not improve society if such ethical reform was "merely incidental to the saving of the souls of lawyers, politicans, business men, and social leaders in another world." The Kingdom of God must be achieved in this world by reforming conditions, and the church must equip people to live ethically and deliver its message in such a way that all could understand it: "Let her preach the gospel as a rule of justification; but she must preach the law as a rule of life, and insist that obedience to it in all the relations of life is the only valid evidence of a saving faith. The epistle of James must be preached as well as those of Paul."[21] He described the church as a largely middle-class institution that ignored the poor. Capitalists and their allies paid their tithes in the belief that contributions absolved them from ethical responsibility for how they earned their money. He did not advocate socialism, arguing that this ideology was not germane. Christ was neither socialist nor antisocialist, he taught neither politics nor economics. But he did teach ethics, which must underlie all political and economic theory. For all Howerton's prophetic prose, however, he was a transitional figure who could not bring himself to advocate a broader social role for the church beyond persuading its members, who in turn must courageously and individually change society.[22]

Although Howerton's book was widely read, its theological arguments made less impact than the practical experiences of Presbyterians. In denominations where the salvation of souls was paramount, structures quickly developed to promote evangelism. One such missionary enterprise slowly evolved in the remote vastness of the Appalachian Mountains. Presbyterians were no strangers to this land for among the early settlers were Scotch-Irish Calvinists who scattered churches throughout the foothills. But further up the hollows and at the higher elevations institutions of all kinds were scarce. The Ladies Board of Missions, PCUSA, established the first denominational school for whites in 1879. Between 1885 and 1895 northern Presbyterians began thirty-one schools and sponsored thirty-four more during the following decade. The PCUS began its mountain work in 1881. The Synod of Kentucky authorized Dr. Edward O. Guerrant of Kentucky to devote his full time to mountain work. Guerrant founded the Society of Soul Winners, also called the American Inland Mission, in 1897 to raise money and recruit home missionaries. Despite its conventional title and Guerrant's passion for saving souls, the society never disengaged from the social workings of mountain life. He had first traveled the mountains as a Confederate soldier and had been impressed with its beauty and the deprivation of its people. As a physician, Guerrant conducted clinics as well as revivals and believed no lasting change could occur in the mountains without education. Beginning with 360 dollars and one mountain missionary in 1897, Guerrant organized the most extensive mission effort in the mountains. He raised in excess of 12,000 dollars each year for more than a decade and supported as many as seventy workers. Although individual salvation never ceased to be his primary goal, he increasingly directed his efforts toward institutional work. In the process he won support of one PCUS agency after another. In 1898 the Asheville Presbytery offered its active support. In 1911 the Executive Committee On Home Missions agreed to sponsor the work. Three years later the Synod of North Carolina proposed a new ecclesiastical jurisdiction for the mountains. Established in 1915, the Synod of Appalachia was created by combining parts of four existing synods (Virginia, Kentucky, North Carolina, and Tennessee).[23]

In time the Society of Soul Winners presided over a far flung network of institutions including Stuart Robinson School at

Blackey, Kentucky (with 18 teachers and 400 pupils), Highland Institute at Guerrant, Kentucky (15 teachers, 200 pupils), Madison Synodical School at Madison, West Virginia (8 teachers, 117 pupils), and Blue Ridge Academy, Hollow, Virginia (6 teachers, 109 pupils). Some of the mountain schools were much more complex than their academic designation suggests. Highland Institute founded in Breathitt County, Kentucky, in 1908 included a church, farm, orphanage, and the only hospital in the county, with a resident physician and nurse. Guerrant regularly took medical personnel with him on trips into remote areas to provide medical care for the destitute people. He frequently conducted medical clinics next to his schools.[24]

Critics of mountain religion have generally dismissed it as traditional, otherworldly Christianity. Mountain preachers seldom preached on ethics and when they did mountain people often resented such references. A visitor during the 1930s heard only one sermon on a social issue and that sermon condemned birth control.[25] But such critics were neither well informed nor even perceptive.

Presbyterians by 1910 had clearly opted for a mixture of spiritual and educational salvation. The PCUS operated mission schools for blacks, immigrants, Indians, and mountain children, but by far the largest effort was in the mountains. Thanks to an individual who contributed 2,000 dollars a year, the Home Mission Board and individual synods were able to expand Guerrant's work. They established schools such as Rabun Gap–Nacoochee in Georgia, Lees–McRae in North Carolina, Grundy in Virginia, Caddo Valley in Arkansas, and School of the Ozarks in Missouri. By 1910 the PCUS sponsored 59 day schools with 1,343 pupils and 239 teachers. Each school combined Bible study and secular education, and most provided industrial/agricultural training for boys and domestic education for girls. The teachers served multiple roles: missionaries, educators, church leaders, social and community workers. The General Assembly considered mountain schools to be "the most important arm in the evangelization of the mountain people. . . ," and the Home Missions committee employed a woman to represent mountain work before synodical Ladies' Societies. By 1914 the annual Home Mission budget for mountain schools had risen to 85,000 dollars, and by 1917 expenditures on the schools exceeded the entire PCUS Home Mission Committee budget of 1907. Mountain work dominated the committee's proceedings; although it created a Subcommittee on Mountain, Mill, City and Country Churches in 1910, its reports to the General Assembly for the next two years dealt exclusively with mountain work.[26]

As Guerrant's health declined, the Home Missions Committee pondered the future of its Appalachian work. The legendary Dr. John C. Campbell, who headed the Southern Highlands Division of the Russell Sage Foundation, was deeply imbued with the Social Gospel and tried to influence the PCUS committee on mountain work to centralize the organization of schools under its jurisdiction. He also sought to minimize sectarianism and encourage interdenominational cooperation. He urged Presbyterians to honor Woodrow Wilson's first wife by creating the Ellen Axson Wilson Memorial Scholarship to support education in Appalachia.[27] His ideas heavily influenced PCUS policy between 1910 and 1920.

The Executive Committee on Home Missions agreed to assume responsibility for the Soul Winners Society in February, 1911, although it employed Dr. Guerrant to oversee the ministry. Almost immediately the committee moved on John C. Campbell's recommendations. It proposed a division of mountain work among Baptists, Methodists, and Presbyterians so as to eliminate duplication. The commitee consolidated mountain activities under a superintendent who administered 50 missionaries and property valued at 49 million dollars, containing 42 mountain schools, 129 teachers, and 3,250 students.[28]

The transition from Guerrant's personal control to coordinated supervision by a committee in Atlanta created problems. William E. Hudson who was appointed superintendent of mountain work became involved in controversy with the Presbytery of West Lexington, Kentucky, when he tried to change the work. The superintendent of Riverside Institute wrote Dr. Guerrant resisting centralization: "none of the members of the Board have had experience enough to enable them to be familiar with the needs, yet they are the real determining factor in matters of government here. . . ."[29] Dr. Guerrant's death in 1916 at age seventy-eight eased tensions somewhat.

Many of the schools became self-supporting and began to disappear in the 1920s and 1930s as public education spread through the mountains. But the Synod of Virginia still supported fifteen mountain schools in the mid 1920s, and the cumulative social impact of Guerrant's four decades of effort was enormous. Beyond the souls saved, thousands of mountain children who otherwise would have grown up illiterate received education. Hundreds of boys and girls unable to pay tuition received scholarships or worked their way through Presbyterian schools. Mollie Clark, a West Virginia coal miner's daughter, was one beneficiary. Her mother and father died when she was nine. She began attending a Presbyterian mission school at Shooting Creek, West Virginia, when she was twelve, was converted at fourteen, and remained at the school for seven years: "At first it was very hard for me to learn. I thought that no one loved me. I lived because I had to, and I wanted to die. When the teachers corrected me . . . I thought they were cruel to me. But with their patience I was convinced that they loved me, and that I was put into the world for a purpose." Later she entered Stonewall Jackson College, working her way through its high school program by serving in a dining room. The Woman's Auxiliary of the PCUS provided a scholarship to help with her expenses. Perhaps part of the money came from Mrs. Woodrow Wilson who took a keen interest in the schools and made a major donation to them. Such testimony emphasizes precisely what Guerrant had intended the schools to do, help Presbyterians convert Appalachian people. But inevitably the schools became more than agents of Presbyterian evangelism. They forced Presbyterians into ecumenical associations and led to conferences for mountain workers from various denominations. They led to the establishment of five PCUS orphanages and several hospitals.[30]

The mountain work also brought Presbyterians into an alien culture where either they had to adapt or force their charges to modify native Appalachian society. Culture shock worked both ways with many teachers disparaging mountain ways even as others followed the example of John and Olive Campbell. Many missionaries could not cope with the strange ways, isolation, and loneliness of the Appalachian frontier. One school teacher who left the Presbyterian school at Crossnore, North Carolina, recommended a classmate from the Presbyterian Training School she thought capable of standing the isolation there. Missionaries to the coal mining camps became agents of Americanization as fully as settlement house workers in Gary, Indiana. The Reverend E. E. Von Peachy, director of work among Hungarians near Holden, West Virginia, visualized his work in apocalyptic terms: "Failure to make Christian Americans out of these ignorant but willing and good Europeans may mean disaster; but success in our frontier work will mean peace, loyalty, faithful citizens of this great country." A pastor from eastern Kentucky desired a more hospitable and civilized environment than Grayson, Kentucky, which he described in the most unflattering terms: "The school is very poor, and I am sure I am not doing our children justice; every housekeeper here, practically, does her own work, it being impossible to employ servants. We have been doing our own work for more than a year, but my wife is not physically able to continue indefinitely."[31]

The same culture shock that drove many Presbyterians from the mountains opened opportunities for others that traditional southern society denied. Dr. Guerrant relied heavily upon women from the outset of his ministry. By 1910 the Society of Soul Winners supported twenty-five women working in the mountains of Kentucky and North Carolina and thirty-five teachers. They came from across America: two women on Turkey Creek in Breathitt County, Kentucky, came from Kansas and Iowa; two teachers at Canoe were North Carolina natives; at Athol the two mountain teachers were from New Jersey; Miss Ella Keigwin from Florida ran Ebenezer Mission in east Tennessee; Miss Alida Beyer of Brooklin resigned her position as a city missionary in New York City to teach children in Kentucky and help carpenters build a church; Miss Mary Robertson of Paris, Texas, directed a mission. Guerrant described the efforts of a female missionary in eastern Kentucky who went to an area without a church, Sabbath school, or preacher, twenty miles from the nearest town or physician to begin a Sunday School. She taught all who came that winter, spreading both the gospel and her short supply of medicines. She took in a woman whose drunken husband had tried to kill her. At the same historical moment that the PCUS east of the mountains adamantly resolved that women should not speak before mixed assemblies of males and females, Guerrant quoted the apostle Paul: "I entreat thee, also, to help those women which labored with me in the Gospel."[32]

The women Guerrant described in his book were indomitable and apparently paid little attention to their previously limited spheres. The gospel had called them to a bold new ministry. Lizzette, whose last name Guerrant did not record, served as a missionary at Glencairn. A graduate of Converse College in South Carolina, she lived alone in a remote cabin, slept in a bed she built herself, taught a school with twenty-four children, and walked more than a hundred miles a month making her rounds. A Presbyterian minister was asked by his missionary daughter, Miss Clemmie Patton of Decatur, Georgia, to preach at the mission she directed in Breathitt, Kentucky. After watching her direct the spiritual activities at the mission, he commented: "Some say that this is irregular; true, but if the work cannot be accomplished in a regular way, it must be done in an irregular way." What the people must have was Christ regardless of the methods. And the women proclaimed a gospel that was liberating in more ways than one. A female missionary described an arduous school regimen, which began at 8:00 a.m. with catechism and Bible verses, followed by religious instruction, and lessons in reading, spelling, mathematics, and geography. After six days of this routine she conducted a Sunday School on the Sabbath. She expressed concern about girls marrying at fourteen or sixteen and tried to broaden "their horizon" so they would not rush into marriage "so thoughtlessly."[33]

The desire to "save" Appalachian girls was a common theme of mountain missionaries. West Virginia missionary O. C. Huston sought a scholarship to the Presbyterian Training School in Richmond for a descendent of the Hatfields, a survivor of the famous feud:

> I really do not know how she will make out, except this, she has the fighting blood of her forebears, and their stubbornness, which will be an asset, if she stands the strain of classroom work. I believe it is worth while to try her, if she will go, for if she comes out all right, she will be just what we need for some of these neighborhoods. . . .[34]

The Training School for Lay Workers, founded in 1914, was the major source of female missionaries and teachers. Many of them took the two-year course of study in Bible, Religious Education, Missions, Personal Work, Christian Doctrine, Church History, Organized Woman's Work, and Social Welfare, then worked in the mountains, mining camps, or urban settlement houses. Women teachers came from quite diverse backgrounds. In 1920 two Vassar College graduates wrote Walter Lingle, who was then president of the Training School, that they wanted to teach in "a rural school in the southern mountains or do some kind of community service or health work." Helen Mathews who wrote Lingle was apparently a Protestant but her companion volunteer was Jewish. Lingle furnished a list of Presbyterian schools.[35]

Once they arrived in the mountains, the women quickly adjusted to unorthodox roles. Mary M. Sloop, principal of Crossnore School in North Carolina, declared war on the county's moonshiners, not that she disliked them personally: "I declare the smartest people on earth are the moonshiners. I just love 'em and they are the best friends I have in the county, even the ones I have arrested. And their children are numberless and as smart as their parents." County revenue agents shirked their duties causing Mrs. Sloop to write: "if I didn't have a family, I'd surely take the job. Am sorter doing it any way, while my careful husband squirms at my audacity." She was determined to locate two Presbyterian missionaries for the moonshine centers of the county, though one suspects her enthusiasm for this ministry exceeded that of her male compatriots. Mrs. Sloop also had an unorthodox notion of women's role in the church. In her attempt to recruit Miss Leyburn, a female missionary, she expressed hope that she could also attract a resident pastor. If so Leyburn's work would not be "so essential to the life of our church. . . ." But pastors were scarce and if none could be found, Leyburn's work would be "that of keeping alive and making to grow a very young and weak little church . . . and . . . if she did not call that a strictly church job, I'd like for her to find one that was."[36]

In the summers many pastors on vacation and theology students visited the mountains to preach, and the women welcomed and deferred to them. But during the hard winters the women led the struggling churches. When the Reverend R. P. Smith explained after one of his sermons that Presbyterians did not have enough ministers to assign them to the mountains on a regular basis, a mountain man responded:

> We like to hear you fellows preach, and I am not saying anything again ye, but if we can't git both, send us the women teachers. These women teach our children books and good manners during the week and on Sunday they teach all of us a lot of what is in the Bible. Tell your folks to send us the teachers, we can git along mighty well for a good while yet just with them doing the work.[37]

Although Edward Guerrant never intended his Society of Soul Winners to expand social opportunities for Presbyterian women or challenge the sexual assumptions of southern society, that was precisely its effect. Nor did he intend for education, orphanages, and health care to assume so large a role in its function, but he endorsed all these goals and without his blessing and assistance, the American Inland Mission would have been nothing more than a series of remote preaching stations.

One reason the Social Gospel in the South has been so easily ignored is that it usually thrived in cities. When interjected into the world of rural America it assumed new directions. The Society of Soul Winners was one such form. The Country Life Movement was another. The progressive vision caught sight of declining rural America during the administration of Theodore Roosevelt. Although the concern was not easily focused, it resulted in numerous conferences, books, and new initiatives to strengthen rural institutions. Virtually all the experts centered their attention on rural schools and churches as the critical institutions in stabilizing farming communities. They recommended that rural sociology be taught in colleges and seminaries, that churches be consolidated, that rural churches become social centers as well as houses of worship, and that congregations build parsonages to attract full-time pastors and eliminate quarter–time and half-time churches.[38] Although the PCUS was not as strong in rural areas as Methodists and Baptists, it developed its own rural brand of the Social Gospel.

The crisis was obvious to all. A Presbyterian in Alabama remembered the decade of the 1890s as one in which PCUS ministers wanted "to leave a country field soon as a city pastorate beckoned." In 1913 the pastor of a small Presbyterian church in Paris, Tennessee, wrote that he could not live on his salary: "I want one single church in a town of good size or in a city." In 1918 the Presbytery of East Mississippi wrote W. L. Lingle that it needed pastors of several "group fields" (multiple churches) in rural areas.[39]

The PCUS began its formal effort to assist country churches almost simultaneous with the first national report on the subject in 1908. The Home Mission Board raised 1,500 dollars to match private contributions of 1,000 dollars to finance a conference for ministers in mountain and rural areas. The board paid expenses for a hundred rural ministers representing several denominations to attend the conference at the Presbyterian assembly grounds at Montreat, North Carolina. Many of the ministers were as poor as the people they served and also lacked education. So successful was the meeting that the board scheduled another in 1910.[40]

One intense but seemingly unlikely observer of this effort was Walter L. Lingle. As pastor of Atlanta's First Presbyterian Church and member of the Home Mission Board, he helped plan the 1910 conference. Unknown to most of his associates, Lingle's commitment to the country church dated back to seminary days when his request for such a parish as his first pastorate had been denied. Destiny had a different fate in store for him. At a strategic moment his visibility as a successful large church pastor and later as a seminary professor placed him as chairman of a committee on the problem of rural pastors for a conference in Chattanooga. Organized by the Southern Conference for Education and Industry, the Chattanooga meeting scheduled for April, 1915, involved many progressive groups, including the Conference of Southern Women, the Southern Educational Council, and the Country Church Conference. The consortium chose the theme of "community," and designated the Reverend A. L. Phillips, general superintendent of the Presbyterian Executive Committee of Publication, to chair the Conference on the Country Church. Phillips asked his friend Lingle to research and recommend strategies for obtaining resident pastors for once-a-month country churches, factors to be considered in the location and construction of church buildings and parsonages, and the church's social and educational role in the community.[41] The Chattanooga meeting meshed nicely with a third PCUS Rural Church Conference planned for Montreat in 1916.

Lingle began preparation for the conferences in 1914. He invited a former student then pastoring a rural church to write an article for the seminary magazine he edited. The pastor, Willis Thompson, from a rural area near Springfield, Kentucky, actually first suggested the 1916 conference because of the serious conditions in rural areas. He had tried to reach the transient population of poor white tobacco farmers, but their tenancy made them so highly mobile that he had serious difficulties. His letter was a composite of condescension and concern:

> Without our numbers there is a welter of tenant tobacco-growers, roving yearly from locality to locality and made up of nominal "Baptists," nominal Campbellites, nominal Methodists, and nominal other things. . . . They are unmanagable and heartbreaking in their resistance . . . to our work. I seem to have won their respect and attention . . . but I shrink from thinking of their carelessness if one who woos them less fondly than I have should have charge of this field. I have learned how to preach to them also; for I won their respect through pastoral work solely. I have to preach so that the better class of people will find stimulus in the sermon and these poor Ishmaelites shall also have fire struck from them. . . . If they would but stay in one place, the task would be simple; I could rejoice in it, for they are sub-soil to my church work. But they rove perpetually.

Thompson attributed his enthusiasm for work among the rural poor to Lingle's guidance: "I had intended to write of what a real stimulus your influence at the Seminary afforded me. . . . It would not be heresy to say that I look eagerly for the modern viewpoint among the brethren in hope that it is with[in] them to back and invigorate the healthy conservatism of our church; but my watching is very discouraging at times."[42]

Thompson's faith in Lingle was not misplaced. Even as he composed his letter, Warren H. Wilson, superintendent of Country Church Work for the PCUSA Board of Home Missions, was advising Lingle about the proper elements to include in a rural church conference. Lingle had not stopped his reading with Walter Rauschenbusch. Another favorite author was Warren Wilson whose research and writing had been inspired by Theodore Roosevelt's 1908 Country Life Commission report. Wilson's books, so eagerly devoured by Lingle, called the church to become a community center. Historically it had been too emotional and individualistic; now it must champion educational improvement and interdenominational cooperation. The major barrier to the spiritual mission of the rural church was not private sin and demonic powers; it was tenancy and rural poverty. In short, Wilson's ideas that so attracted Lingle expanded the Social Gospel into a rural setting.[43] When Lingle wrote Wilson for advice on the Chattanooga and Montreat conferences, the PCUSA minister responded enthusiastically and at length. He recommended that only pastors of small struggling rural churches be invited, and suggested from his experience that the most popular courses would be in "Social Religion," the "Church and Community" or "Religious Sociology," and another in "Religious Pedagogy" or "The Teaching of Religion." He advised that the faculty be recruited from agricultural colleges and state universities; "I do not think that the school [conference] ought to become a place for missionary secretaries, or temperance advocates, or Sabbath observance exponents, or any other propagandists to tell their cause. . . ." Finally, the conference would have to pay the expenses of the rural ministers. Lingle was so impressed with Wilson's advice that he invited the northern Presbyterian to help him draft a "platform," which became the basis of Lingle's session at the Chattanooga conference.[44]

The July, 1916, Montreat Conference on the Country Church allowed Lingle to develop his philosophy more fully. As the conference's organizer, he presented daily lectures on "The Social Teachings of the Bible," a topic that had come to dominate his teaching as well as his sermons. He also recruited the Reverend W. H. Mills, a professor of Rural Sociology at Columbia Theological Seminary and Clemson College and a specialist on the problems of country churches, to lecture each day. Lingle was so impressed by the applied Christianity of Mills that he also printed the professor's essays on the rural church in the *Union Seminary Review.*[45]

Lingle's advocacy of the Social Gospel in the country did not detract from his continuing interest in the urban South. From the vantage point of Atlanta, Lingle saw the problems created by a rapidly expanding city. He and a layman proposed in 1908 that the city's Sunday School Union purchase ten acres on the outskirts of Atlanta and construct a recreation center with tennis courts, a baseball diamond, croquet grounds, swimming pool, and picnic facilities. It should be located on a trolley line so Atlanta's children would have access to it. Such a development would indicate that the Sunday School cared for the "social and physical welfare of its members as well as for the spiritual." He also fought to prevent his congregation from selling their downtown site and moving the church to the suburbs. It was partly Lingle's involvement with urban problems that led to his appointment as a member of the PCUS Home Mission Board.[46]

The board was the PCUS agency most involved with the changing course of urban society. Its attempts to evangelize the city ran head on into new realities. The board's urban initiatives resulted partly from threats to traditional values. It defined its task as fitting the one million immigrants entering the United States each year "for intelligent citizenship." The "representatives of anarchy and atheism from the old world are organizing schools where their views are taught to their children. They combine together to root up every Christian and religious element from our educational system, and many of the Jewish population are joining them." As part of their strategy, the Home Mission Committee proposed hiring Christian teachers and requiring prayer in public schools.[47]

Coercion alone could not solve the problem, however, so the Home Mission Board sought other strategies as well. Between 1908 and 1915 the board sponsored work among immigrants in a number of southern cities, including Tampa, Birmingham, New

Orleans, and El Paso. It worked with other denominations to share responsibility. The board organized subcommittees to work with blacks, immigrants, Indians, mountain people, mill workers, the country church, and city missions.[48]

As with most southerners, progressive Presbyterians did little to improve race relations. The Home Mission Committee recommended the establishment of a segregated black synod in 1915. The Woman's Auxiliary supported the work of black Presbyterians at Stillman College in Alabama and raised substantial funds for the school. The director of the Woman's Auxiliary, Hallie Winnsborough, took an active interest in blacks and supported the Commission on Interracial Cooperation, though she despaired at its excessive caution. Under her leadership, PCUS women sponsored conferences on race relations at the level of both presbytery and synod, capped by an annual summer conference at Stillman College in Tuscaloosa.[49]

Walter Lingle tried to improve race relations in Atlanta, a city infamous for anti-Negro violence and lynching during the first two decades of the century. Together with the pastor of the First Congregational Church, he proposed creation of a reformatory for black boys funded by public taxes as a way of separating them from prison and the convict lease system. Just as Warren Wilson was his inspiration on the country church and Walter Rauschenbusch on the Social Gospel, Marjorie Gray was a formative influence on his racial views. She was a northern woman who traveled South to teach at Atlanta University. She attended First Presbyterian Church where she listened intently to his sermons dealing with social issues. But she waited in vain to hear him address racial injustice. In a series of letters to him she communicated her disappointment and tried to educate him about conditions in the city. She described racial insults to black faculty and students at the university and told him that respectable black women feared for the morals of their daughters who worked as servants in the homes of whites. She also sent him essays by W. E. B. DuBois to read. Apparently her efforts succeeded.[50] In subsequent years Lingle became a leading advocate of desegregation in the Presbyterian church. But with progressive leaders such as Alexander McKelway so locked into a racist culture, these reforms were delayed for decades.

Other aspects of the urban Social Gospel became the subject of a major debate within the PCUS. Leading the forces of change was Walter Lingle. A native of Rowan County, North Carolina, and graduate of a denominational college and seminary, he was an ideal spokesman for social service. He read widely and kept his mind open to new theological concepts. He held a succession of important positions: pastor of Atlanta's First Presbyterian Church, professor of Christian sociology at Union Seminary, editor of the *Union Theological Review,* columnist for the *Presbyterian of the South* and the *Christian Observer,* president of the Layman's Training School in Richmond and later of Davidson College. These provided Lingle platforms from which he influenced the thinking and course of the denomination. Social activism was only one dimension of his ministry, a fact that aided him in battles with conservatives. Although he was devoted to social Christianity, conservatives respected him for his good judgment, opposition to alcohol and divorce, and hard work as a member of numerous agencies and boards. Northern churchmen found him a bit out of step before 1910. When he submitted an essay on Calvin to *The Interior* published in Chicago, the editor turned it down. His readers were "so heartily tired of Calvin that I really think a return to the subject some time later might be more efficient. Besides, a modern newspaper finds that it must indulge in history sparingly. The demand on it is for something up to date." The Atlanta pastor was not so out of touch with "up to date" matters as the editor might have thought. Rauschenbusch's ideas had already taken hold. Historian Ernest Thompson summarized Lingle best: he was "never so far in advance of the church that he could not gain a hearing but always far enough to broaden the church's viewpoint. . . ."[51]

When Lingle left Atlanta for Union Seminary in 1911 he entered the most influential phase of his ministry. His duties included teaching the new course in sociology authorized by the 1911 General Assembly. No such course had been taught previously, and he received numerous letters concerning its content. One Presbyterian minister wrote supportively that it was far better for a young theologian "to know something about the housing conditions of Richmondites than to be intimately acquainted with the family life of the Hittites; the Richmondites being still alive, and the Hittites having been a long time dead." Other ministers equated sociology and socialism and opposed both. Some were just confused. A prominent Presbyterian woman with six daughters thought the course was wonderful because her daughters could clarify their views on cards, theaters, and dancing.[52]

Lingle defined the course as an orientation to social service such as Christ had performed among the multitudes, an attempt to "translate into life the social and ethical teachings of our Lord." He rejected alike individualism, socialism, and communism as ways to solve social problems. The Christian ideal of social service worked best but was opposed both by conservatives who believed that Christianity contained no social message and by liberals who found nothing in the Bible except a social message. He proposed a middle position. He believed that the Kingdom of God was used in many ways in the Bible but one emphasized its earthly aspects. Although Rauschenbusch influenced him more than other theologians and ethicists, he frequently cited Shailer Mathews and Josiah Strong. His reading extended well beyond these three, however, and usually found its way into his courses, sermons, and correspondence. He read W. M. Clow's Social Gospel book, *Christ in the Social Order,* as a possible text for his course, and borrowed a thesis entitled "Marxian Socialism and the Bible" written by a young Presbyterian student at the University of Chicago.[53]

Students felt his imprint. A young Presbyterian missionary in a remote area of Alaska clearly bore Lingle's ideological stamp. He criticized a Congregational missionary for his "soothing syrup, socialism and social service that makes me tired. If a man is drowning he does not want a bottle of milk, he wants a life preserver. . . ." But the former student championed "the value of social service for it has its place, one which the Church in the past has failed to give it. . . . Have enjoyed reading Rauschenbusch's 'Social Principles of Jesus X'." To his request for further reading about socialism, Lingle recommended a balanced list including H. C. Vedder's *Socialism and the Ethics of Jesus*, John Spargo's *Socialism*, Arthur J. Balfour's *The Case Against Socialism*, and Father Barnard Vaughan's *Socialism From the Christian's Standpoint.*[54]

Almost as important as his classroom was editorship of the *Union Theological Review*. He turned that journal into a forum on the Social Gospel. He reviewed current and controversial books by all major Social Gospel figures as well as Warren Wilson's works on the country church. He organized series dealing with social issues, including one on the proper role of the church in society. Because of the intense debate within the PCUS on the social message of the church, he asked moderators of the northern and southern churches to respond to his question "What is the business of the Church?"[55]

As a lecturer, preacher, and essayist, Lingle gained even more attention within the church. His sermon manuscripts are preoccupied with social problems, especially unjust economic conditions, and his favorite source was Walter Rauschenbusch. In a sermon entitled "The Bible and Money," he traced America's social problems to the accumulation of vast wealth in the hands of a few individuals. The accumulation produced two problems: an idle class of rich and social unrest among the poor. Money was not inherently bad, but abuses of money such as paying unfair wages were evil. Lingle also rejected the notion of a market economy: "We are too apt to let the wage scale be determined by the laws of political economy, and not by the teachings of Christ." His sermon on "Wealth and Social Problems" was more specific. He cited 1916 income tax data showing the incomes of the nine richest men and a wide disparity in wealth between them and the rest of society. The problem was the concentration of power to control money markets, prices, and wages, a condition that created social unrest. He summarized Christ's teachings about wealth and treatment of the poor using Rauschenbusch's book *Christianity and the Social Crisis* as a source. As an example of proper Christian stewardship, he cited his Atlanta friend, John J. Eagan, a Presbyterian layman who had shocked the business world by allowing his workers to elect the Board of Operators and share company profits. Lingle attributed poverty to a multiplicity of sources: war, drunkenness, sloth, improvidence, ignorance, physical or mental defectiveness, crime, and dishonesty; but he also traced it to environment, industrial oppression, changing technology, and inadequate wages. The Bible denounced those who oppressed or neglected the poor and taught that the Church as a corporate body should provide for them. But he proposed no specific strategies to correct economic abuses except the application of private ethics and the collective involvement of the church in caring for the poor.[56]

Although he devoted less attention to other subjects, he did not ignore them altogether. In his sermon on "The Family and Social Problems" he attributed blame for faltering marriages and disintegrating families not only to drunkenness and immorality, but to child labor, tenement houses, and slums. His discussion on "Christianity and the Race Problem" raised a series of extremely troubling questions for southerners:

> Is our treatment of the Negro Christian? Do we know the Negro, especially the educated Negro? Should Negroes receive equal treatment with the Whites in respect to schools, courts, housing, streets, sanitation, travel, etc.? Would Jesus draw the color line in His Church? How shall we treat Negro delegates and commissioners who attend Church meeting and General Assemblies? Should Negroes be entertained in hotels with the Whites at meetings of the Pan-Presbyterian Council and other similar religious gatherings?[57]

Such sermons and lectures increased his popularity. Invitations to preach poured into his Richmond office, often with requests for specific sermons on Christianity and social problems. One Presbyterian minister engaged in the ultimate form of flattery after reading Lingle's sermon on "The Teachings of Jesus and Modern Social Problems." He decided to preach it himself.[58] The president of the North Carolina Conference for Social Service invited Lingle to address the organization's fourth annual state conference in 1916. The Charlotte, North Carolina, Ministerial Association recommended that the city's pastors preach the Sunday morning of the conference on Christian Social Service. That evening they planned a combined service to hear Lingle preach. Conference officials asked the seminary professor to refute the "current opinion that there is a sort of conflict or incompatibility between individual Christianity and social Christianity." Lingle gladly accepted, offering a choice of three sermons that would fit the themes. From the National Board of the Y.M.C.A. came a request to lecture at the Southern Student's Conference on Christianity about the world crisis of 1918. The National Chautauqua invited him to lecture nationwide on the social teachings of Jesus and contemporary problems.[59]

Editors also sought his essays. He popularized most of his writings for Presbyterian newspapers and Sunday School literature. In 1916 the editor of *The Westminster Teacher* asked Lingle to prepare a series of lessons for the quarterly on "The Social Teachings of the Bible." He wanted the lessons to provoke discussion, not lead to "yes" or "no" answers.[60]

But Lingle's best known publication was a collection of papers delivered as the James Sprunt Lectures at Union Theological Seminary in 1929. Published under the title *The Bible and Social Problems,* they contained basically the same material he disseminated so widely in sermons between 1915 and 1920, though presented in a more systematic way. Chapters on "The Bible and Poverty" came directly from his sermon. But his essay on "The Church and Social Reform" was more pointed and direct. Ministers must study the social problems of their communities and then preach about those problems from the pulpit, not to engage in partisan politics but in order to apply the social and ethical teachings of Christ. Church courts should deal with conflicts between labor and capital as well as with private ethical matters. They must define clearly which of Christ's teachings governed labor and which management, because "Jesus' ideal for the world is that the Kingdom of God should come on earth as it has already come in heaven."[61]

Although Walter Lingle was the most influential Social Gospel spokesman within the PCUS, he was by no means a voice crying in the wilderness. A. W. McAllister, a prominent businessman and moderator of Orange Presbytery, opened the 1914 meeting with an address urging churches to pay more attention to social problems. As a result of too much emphasis on individual aspects of religion, workingmen were ignored and were leaving the church. That same year, the Reverend Stonewall J. McMurry, speaking at Austin Seminary in Texas, warned that the church could not ignore the injustice of wages and the maldistribution of wealth. A. M. Scales, ruling elder in Greensboro, North Carolina, and a former governor of the state, argued that Presbyterians would attract unchurched people if they were more committed to social service.[62]

So long as such advice was directed at individual members, even conservatives within the PCUS could agree. The General Assembly in 1914 adopted a report drafted by a joint committee of the PCUS, PCUSA, and the Associated Reformed Presbyterian Church on the relationship of the church to social reform. The report urged members to practice Christian principles in all social relations, encouraged the creation of voluntary organizations devoted to social reform, and recommended the Federal Council of Churches of Christ in America as a cooperative vehicle for Christian social service. Conservative Presbyterians did not object to that portion of the report urging individual members to action, but they did oppose the Federal Council.[63]

The debate was soon joined by Presbyterians who believed that individual action, efficacious though it might be, could not dramatically change complex social institutions. They proposed to organize Presbyterian institutions in such a way as to alter urban life. Their campaigns against child labor and alcohol had already won them allies among moderates, but now the boldest pastors and laymen proposed more sweeping changes. The development of institutional churches among Presbyterians began as part of the Home Mission Board effort to reach immigrants. Plagued by illiteracy, poor housing, inadequate medical services, lack of child care and recreational facilities, immigrants had more immediate concerns than the welfare of their souls. Often Catholic in background and preoccupied by "this worldly" problems, they did not frequent Presbyterian churches. The Home Mission Board sought to reach them by a ministry more balanced between spiritual and physical needs. In 1910 it planned an institutional church for immigrants in El Paso and for blacks in Louisville that would offer a variety of social services. With the cooperation of Central Presbyterian Church in Kansas City, the board began an institutional church for the city's 6,000 Italians. Begun in 1908, it had a kindergarten, sewing school, boys' and girls' clubs, cooking and English classes, as well as preaching services. Institutional work among Italians in Birmingham was even more developed. Presbyterians organized a settlement house at Ensley, Alabama, under the direction of an Italian pastor and American social workers. The pastor conducted a night school, preached, and conducted Bible study. The women taught a kindergarten with seventy students from five nationalities. The Woman's Missionary Union in the city paid part of their salaries. Miss Agnes Averyt taught a night school at the settlement house and directed domestic science classes and boys' and mothers' clubs. Presbyterians also rented a house in the industrial suburb of Pratt City where Miss Ramelle Anderson opened a day school and conducted other social ministries. Similar work was begun among Cubans in Tampa and Hungarians in St. Petersburg. Sometimes the work prospered as in Pratt City, and at other times vigorous Catholic opposition stopped it as in Ensley.[64]

Although the PCUS did not become as deeply committed to settlement houses and institutional churches as Methodists, enthusiasm for such ministries did spread. In 1910 a church leader proposed to W. L. Lingle that First Presbyterian Church in Atlanta become the foundation for a "great Institutional Church" like Wesley Memorial Church in the city. He proposed attaching a Presbyterian hospital and various social service agencies to the church.[65] Lingle left Atlanta months later, so nothing came of the proposal, but he did take the idea with him to Union Seminary, which was a fertile climate for such notions.

Presbyterian seminaries were not unaware of the new theological currents surging through America. The PCUS Committee on Theological Seminaries urged curriculum innovations to accommodate the new ideas. Not only did Union employ Lingle to teach Christian sociology, but other seminaries quickly followed suit. The Presbyterian Theological Seminary of Kentucky added four new courses in 1915—Christian Sociology, Christian Ethics, Religious Education, and Christian Missions. Columbia Theological Seminary employed an expert in rural sociology and established a chair of Christian Ethics and Apologetics.[66]

Because the primary emphasis of the seminaries was theological, applied ethics and practical training for social service did not attract great interest. Consequently in 1911 the General Assembly created a special committee to investigate the possibility of a school for lay people. The committee, headed by the Reverend H. H. Sweets of Louisville who was deeply involved in the mountain work, reported that the denomination badly needed assistant pastors, Sunday School superintendents, teachers, nurses, and social workers, but had no institution to train them. In 1914 the General Assembly created the Training School at Richmond and established a curriculum consisting both of traditional courses (English Bible, Church History, Presbyterian Standards, Home and Foreign Missions) and innovative ones (City Missions, Day Nursery, Country Church).[67] Under W. L. Lingle's presidency the Training School staffed most of the Social Gospel agencies of the denomination, including its settlement houses, institutional churches, and mountain schools.

Church conferences at Montreat also popularized the Social Gospel. In addition to summer conferences devoted to the country church, the annual Home Missions Conference typically dealt with social ministries. The 1917 session featured programs on Stillman College, West Virginia coal miners, and mountain schools. W. L. Lingle frequently led Bible study on some aspect of Christianity and social problems.[68]

Concrete results of such courses and conferences can only be inferred. But individual churches, presbyteries, and synods did organize interesting new ministries. The First Presbyterian Church of Roanoke, Virginia, established a mission in the cotton mill village with a church building and "annex for social work." In 1914 the pastor asked Lingle for the name of a student who could direct the ministry. A pastor in Concord, North Carolina, addressed a similar inquiry to Lingle a year later. The First Presbyterian Church had sponsored a mission church in the mill village that was nearly self-supporting. He believed that the new pastor "must be one of or with" the textile people to be successful. In 1917 First Presbyterian of Gastonia, North Carolina, sought an assistant pastor to take charge of work in the mill village. The Gastonia congregation, however, was not so anxious that the new pastor identify with the workers. The president of the mill was an officer in First Presbyterian and would provide his support, which lent special meaning to the pastor's request that the student have "practical judgment and horse sense." These inquiries especially interested Lingle. He had once pastored in Rock Hill, South Carolina, which contained a number of mills. At a ministers' meeting he had suggested that the Baptists, Methodists, and Presbyterians divide the villages, with each assuming responsibility for specific areas. All ministers endorsed the proposal enthusiastically except one Baptist preacher who blocked the joint venture. When Lingle returned many years later, all three denominations had rival churches in each mill village, all of them weak and inefficient. That experience left Lingle committed to ecumenical cooperation in church ministries.[69]

Such local concerns seemed minor as international tensions increased. Although antiwar sentiment is often associated with liberalism, conservatives within the PCUS were strangely ambivalent and divided on the issues of war and peace. In 1912 the editor of the *Presbyterian Standard,* one of the most influential and conservative journals, condemned war:

> It is a hopeful sign of the times that Christians are lifting a more united voice against war. . . . the Christian is pledged to keep out of it, and, so far as in him lies, to keep everybody else out of it. No Christian parent should send a son to West Point or Annapolis. Why should boys of Christian households be taught the art of making hell.[70]

One explanation for such advice from a conservative Presbyterian weekly was the doctrine of the spirituality of the church. As the United States drifted into the First World War, federal officials sought to mobilize churches on behalf of the war effort. It was not a difficult task because Christians were caught up in the chauvinism of the times. But Presbyterians absolutely committed to denying the church a formal voice in issues of public policy extended their doctrine to the war. As with social questions in general, Presbyterians disagreed on this crisis. When a Wilmington, North Carolina, pastor proposed to display the American flag in his church, the *Presbyterian Standard* rejected the practice as inappropriate. The editor reminded his readers that during the Civil War northern Presbyterians had displayed the American flag whereas southern churches had refused to unfurl the Confederate ensign. Southern Presbyterians believed that separation of church and state should be absolute. When the church covered the pulpit with the nation's flag it proclaimed itself an ally of the state, an alliance both unholy and unscriptural. But many Presbyterians wrote the paper objecting to this position. International affairs caused the editor no small amount of doctrinal trouble. When some Presbyterians chided the Federal Council of Churches for sending a delegation to Paris in 1919 on behalf of the League of Nations, the editors of the *Standard* defended the council by arguing that some political questions contained "a legitimate moral side" that allowed the church to speak.[71]

Perhaps the confusion of the *Presbyterian Standard* reflected the divisions among Presbyterians concerning the justice and morality of war. The Lingle family was deeply divided on this issue. Walter Lingle reluctantly supported the war. His brother Thomas, a professor at Davidson College, was so enthusiastic a supporter of the allies that he volunteered to serve as a YMCA representative with the American Expeditionary Force in France. But a third brother, W. H. Lingle, who was serving as a missionary in China, thought the war iniquitous. He and Thomas conducted such an acrimonious debate that it destroyed their relationship. He had read many books sent by his brothers in an effort to justify the war: "but they have not convinced me, and there is no book that can convince me. I do not believe Christianity and war are reconcilable, and I hold to Christianity. I do not believe that Jesus Christ would approve war under any circumstances." Americans must put Christ above Theodore Roosevelt and Woodrow Wilson, he wrote, and he doubted Wilson could have been elected had the people known he would lead them into war. His daughters, both students in America, violently disagreed with him. Margaret wrote her uncle that she did not understand how her father could be so "absolutely pro-German after all they have done." But her father held his ground, relieved that though his daughters were caught up in America's "war madness," at least he had no sons to become "cannon fodder."[72]

The war and his family's division about its morality made a profound impression on W. L. Lingle. In his 1929 Sprunt Lectures he devoted an entire essay to "The Bible and War." He traced its causes to class, racial, and national hatred, greed, selfishness, yellow journalism, national chauvinism, and the glorification of war. Because God's ideal was peace, the church should preach against such forces. It must actively seek righteousness and justice between nations.[73]

War and its aftermath also partly explain the increasing conservatism within the PCUS. In 1919 immigration threatened to overwhelm the country. Strikes, social conflict, and disorder spread fear and nativism among the middle class. The 1919 General Assembly, discussing the implications of the postwar world, warned that the church must convert and Americanize the new wave of immigrants. The alternative was ominous: "If Bolshevism, the labor question and the race problem should form a coalition, Christian civilization itself will tremble in the balance."[74]

The real challenge to the fundamental structure of American society did not emanate from radical conspiracies of workers, political radicals, and blacks, as Presbyterians believed. It was more subtle and close to home and its source was American women.

The saga of Presbyterian women between 1900 and 1920 reveals the complex interaction of Christianity and culture. Denominational women could not escape involvement with the secular issues of their times: feminism, divorce, birth control, middle-class rebellion, women's suffrage, and working women.

No denomination more adamantly resisted expanding the role of women. James Woodrow, a professor at Columbia Theological Seminary, decried the "perversion of women's influence" evidenced by "male women, female lecturers, public speakers and preachers, and all 'woman's rights' advocates." The same year, Robert L. Dabney, professor at Union Theological Seminary in Richmond, opposed women as preachers or teachers and castigated southern ministers for allowing women a larger sphere in church life. The year of this "abomination" was 1879. In 1897 the West Lexington Presbytery inquired of the General Assembly whether women should be allowed to speak before a mixed audience containing men. The Assembly cited the Old School Assembly of 1832 and the General Assembly of 1872, both of which approved meetings of pious women to talk and pray but cited both I Corinthians and I Timothy as prohibiting women from teaching, exhorting, or leading prayer in "public and promiscuous assemblies."[75]

Even attempts by southern Presbyterian women to organize missionary societies met stiff resistance. Denominational leaders attacked the societies as efforts to displace the organized church without scriptural authority, to provide undue prominence to one phase of church work to the injury of others, and to obscure the unity of the church. The Synod of Virginia offered more clearly anti-feminist reasons. In 1899 it issued a report misnamed the rights and duties of women, misnamed because it dwelt on duties and listed few rights:

> the woman was created out and for the man. . . . The first law of government is, 'thy desire shall be unto thy husband, and he shall rule over thee'. . . .
> The family, the home, is by the Scriptures made the special sphere of woman . . . 'wandering from house to house' characterizes those on whom the censure of the Holy Spirit falls heavily. . . . The home and the family, the last and strongest bulwark of society, of the state and of the church, the 'Woman's Movement' tends to undermine and destroy.[76]

When the General Assembly finally allowed the creation of separate female organizations, the Standing Committee on Women's Societies, consisting of twelve males, recommended that the Women's Missionary Union be placed under the control of the presbytery. In that way the Presbyterian W.M.U., unlike the Southern Baptist equivalent, was not autonomous and did not control its own finances.[77]

Contact with more enlightened regions did little to alter the minds of male southern Presbyterians. A former member of

W. L. Lingle's church staff in Atlanta moved to Central Presbyterian Church in Denver, Colorado. The church had a sharp-tongued Scottish pastor and a woman secretary-treasurer. During one of the Reverend McNeill's Wednesday evening sermons in 1915 a woman interrupted him and spoke to the congregation at length, after which McNeill raged at that "fool American woman" who "didn't hesitate to drag her confounded impertinence right into the holy of holies." That incident was sufficient to convince the transplanted southerner:

> These western women are so ugly and as they vote here in Colorado there is no abiding with them. They take such a hand in church affairs. Every church business affair I preside over there are the women to deal with. If I ever have a church no woman shall even lift a voice in affairs. . . . by all means oppose voting for women.[78]

Presbyterian women listened to such diatribes but paid them little heed. By 1900 they had organized 1,000 missionary societies and 30 presbyterial unions. In 1904 the Synod of Texas allowed the first synodical union for women. But they still were embarrassed at how poorly developed their work was compared to other denominations. Hallie Winsborough, a Kansas City housewife with six children, decided to change that situation. In her quiet but determined way she won support in the Missouri Synod for a woman secretary for Home and Foreign Missions. Opposition to the proposal came mainly from east of the Mississippi. The Reverend M. L. Lambdin of Montgomery, West Virginia, wrote an article for the *Presbyterian Standard* arguing that the proposal undermined the conservative and scriptural position of the PCUS. He denounced it because women already had enough influence and because it was part of the "rapidly growing evils and ominous signs of the times. . . . the widespread feminine sex unrest." This was a "neurotic species of disease, that renders the unhappy victim . . . discontented with her divinely ordained sex limitations" and led to a rationalistic denial of Bible teachings on "the priority of man and subordination of woman in the home, the church, and the state." Other Presbyterian males were less restrained. They referred to the proposed secretary as "unwomanly," "a limited pope," "a woman bishop," "an ecclesiastical suffragette."[79]

Surprisingly, most church leaders supported the appointment, demonstrating the change in attitudes that was occurring. The *Presbyterian Standard* printed articles on both sides of the issue, one of which took a more liberal view of Timothy and Corinthians and reminded church members that Phoebe had served the New Testament church and surely must have spoken in the presence of males. The author opposed ordaining women as ministers or elders but conceded their right to teach a mixed class, pray, prophesy, serve as a deacon, or even "preach the Gospel." He urged men to "help women of our church who labor in the Gospel" and give them a general secretary for woman's work if they wanted one. His view prevailed. The Executive Committee approved the request from Mrs. Winsborough at its January 9, 1912, meeting, and the General Assembly concurred at its annual gathering.[80]

The choice as first Superintendent of the Woman's Auxiliary was both obvious and fortuitous. Mrs. W. C. Winsborough presided from headquarters in Kansas City. She organized a Woman's Council composed of women presidents of synodical groups and proved amazingly effective as a fund raiser for Presbyterian causes. The first full year of operation, 1913, the Woman's Auxiliary raised 74,000 dollars for missions. So successful were the efforts of women that the 1914 General Assembly urged pastors and sessions to encourage women's societies and each presbytery and synod to appoint a permanent committee on women's work. Unfortunately the Assembly did not change its practice of taking all the money women raised, then parceling a portion back to support their work. Like W. L. Lingle, Mrs. W. C. Winsborough was conservative enough to make her social views palatable to a traditional denomination. When Lingle asked her to recommend a female principal for one of the training

schools, Winsborough carefully qualified her recommendation of
Miss Barbara Lambdin of Berry School in north Georgia. Lambdin had proper qualifications but:

> Of course, I believe very strongly that no woman reaches the
> full development of her powers who has not been wife and
> mother. These experiences give her understanding and sym-
> pathy, a comprehension of problems and ability to handle them
> which comes to women in no other way. However, the wives
> and mothers who are in position to take such work, during
> their middle years are few and I feel sure you do not want an
> old lady as they reckon old ladies now days Miss Lambdin is a
> woman of rare spirituality. Is older than she appears and has
> been a teacher.[81]

Such traditional views allowed her to effectively expand the
influence of women within the PCUS without causing a backlash
among males. By 1919 there were 2,347 women's societies with
65,405 members. Together they contributed 565,000 dollars to
missions. Women studied for mission work in PCUS seminaries
and constituted a substantial proportion of students at the training school in Richmond. In 1913 Austin Seminary in Texas en-
rolled twenty-seven men studying for the ministry and three
women preparing for foreign missions. More significantly PCUS
schools, churches, settlement houses, and agencies actively recruited women for jobs. In 1918 the Home Mission Committee
asked Lingle to recommend a female graduate of the training
school to work in the settlement house at Ensley, Alabama, for a
salary of fifty dollars per month plus a room. The pastor of Independent Presbyterian Church in Savannah, Georgia, planned
new work and needed a senior seminary student *or* a woman
from the Training School with missionary spirit and the capacity
to hold prayer meetings and direct Sunday School. But his liberation was only partial. If he employed a woman, he added, she
should be capable of doing stenographic work and looking after
the office in the mornings. Despite such limitations, women
were charting a new course within the denomination. In 1917

two women were elected trustees of the training school, the first women ever selected for such a position. Three years later women were added to all executive committees. Also in 1920 Mrs. Winsborough, with only one dissenting vote, was invited to address the General Assembly on behalf of the Women's Auxiliary. Although it may seem a small victory in retrospect, the invitation thrilled Hallie Winsborough, who must have remembered twenty years earlier when PCUS policy prohibited women from addressing "a mixed assemblage."[82]

Such victories did not come easily. After 1912 reluctant male Presbyterians contested every forward step taken by women, making female progress all the sweeter.

In some churches women sought to organize societies and men tried to prevent them. A church that met at Union Theological Seminary in Richmond and contained many faculty families instructed its women's society to withdraw from the Presbyterial Union. Leaders of the session contended that the General Assembly's plan for women's societies encouraged females to speak before mixed assemblages. They cited three women who advocated the plan publicly as the logical consequence of such initiatives. The congregation was badly split, with some seminary faculty fearing the session's action would make the seminary appear reactionary. At each annual General Assembly resolutions were proposed condemning the more liberal position taken on "woman's position in the Church," almost always citing I Corinthians 14 and I Timothy 2 as authority for silencing women in the church. In each case the General Assembly's action reaffirmed the position of the 1880 Assembly, which had rejected ordination for women but left other issues to "the discretion of the Sessions and the enlightened consciences of our Christian women themselves." Although women were excluded from the presbytery, they were allowed to hold the office of deacon.[83]

The *Presbyterian Standard* maintained a neutral stance concerning the decision to recommend a woman superintendent, but it soon returned to a more conservative stance. In 1918 the

journal attacked the Methodists and Baptists for extending representation to women, arguing that the logical result of such action
would be ordaining women to preach. Presbyterian women had
not yet disparaged the Apostle Paul "but they show symptoms.
They will be heard from by and by. Paul was an Old School
Presbyterian and that kind is getting scarce." The editor had to
wait less than four months for the assault. He had an explanation
for why aggressive women disliked Paul: "Simply because he
tried to get self-assertive and obstreperous women to behave
themselves in church and married women to recognize the husband as head of the house. For these well-meant efforts of his,
some women can never forgive him." The editor also opposed
woman suffrage. In a particularly ugly editorial, he discussed
Frederick Douglass and Elizabeth Cady Stanton. He described
Douglass as "a negro with a white wife" who favored woman
suffrage and social equality. He hinted darkly that when female
suffrage leaders visited Douglass they went for long private walks
with him in the garden. Stanton wrote a "Woman's Bible" and
denied the divinity of Christ. Current leaders of the suffrage
movement meddled with social questions and dabbled in politics. They sneered at religion, belittled the home, encouraged
marriage outside the sanction of the church, and supported divorce. And even "good and pure" women were joining their
cause.[84]

One such woman was Clara Lingle, wife of Thomas W. and
sister-in-law of W. L. Lingle. A gifted speaker, she became
deeply involved in all phases of the woman's movement. She
participated in the North Carolina Federation of Women's Clubs
and the North Carolina Conference for Social Service. In 1915
she traveled to Raleigh where she and Dr. Anna Howard Shaw
addressed the legislature on behalf of woman suffrage. Her husband supported her completely, often accompanied her on speaking trips, and even tallied audience size and reaction. When her
husband volunteered for YMCA service with the AEF in France,
she moved the children to Chapel Hill where she became advisor

to the Division for Women, Bureau of Extension, at the University of North Carolina. Her assignments included lecturing to women's groups, correspondence, and preparation of study outlines on female welfare and education. In many ways the job was a continuation of the volunteer work she had performed for six years. She remained active in Presbyterian affairs, participating in the Chapel Hill church and teaching a course in parliamentary law for the 1918 Woman's Summer School of Missions.[85]

Although the two Lingle brothers applauded her work, her liberation complicated her husband's life. In 1916 students at Davidson College denounced T. W. Lingle as a teacher. They accused him of sarcasm, unfairness, and pedantry, among other failings. Davidson's president confronted Lingle about his alleged inadequacies and warned him that he must improve or face dismissal. But Lingle claimed his real problem was two or three people "who cannot tolerate in this town a woman who has attained to the prominence, popularity and service all over North Carolina that Clara has." The simplest way to rid themselves of his wife was to "magnify my faults and weaknesses and get rid of me." Whether a rationalization of his own inadequacies or a genuine example of Presbyterian sexism, the incident did demonstrate the marital tensions that accompanied the attempt of Presbyterian women to establish separate identities.[86]

W. L. Lingle demonstrated the same commitment to women's rights as on all social questions. In his sermons on the family written during this era, he emphasized the revolt of women. Perhaps thinking of his sister-in-law Clara, he discussed their role in business, the professions, society, and politics. He called for a calm and careful rethinking of women's roles, discussed both the Bible's teachings on women and the feminist movement, then told his congregation that "Jesus evidently placed women on an equality with man." But he could not bring himself to endorse the ordination of women. A young North Carolina pastor wrote that his session had appointed two deaconesses and inquired about the proper procedure for installing them. The session desired to ordain them. Lingle was "pleased to see how progressive and up-to-date your Church Session is" and endorsed the selection of deaconesses. But to ordain them would be contrary to the Book of Church Order and the provisions of the General Assembly. He proposed instead a public installation of the deaconesses without ordination. In a sermon on "Poverty and Social Problems," Lingle proposed that churches appoint a committee of deacons to assist the poor, then added almost as an afterthought in his sermon notes, "might add deaconesses." But as late as 1925 he believed the PCUS would "unite unanimously on the idea that we will have no women preachers or elders." Beyond that one restriction, however, the PCUS had reached no consensus. Indeed, the issue was so heated in 1915 that when Lingle sought articles for the *Union Seminary Review* on "The Place and Work of Women in the New Testament Church," one minister he asked to write an essay replied: "Did I not know that you were a very amiable man and a lover of your brethren, I might suspect you of trying to get some of us into trouble. This is certainly a thorny subject. I . . . am not at all sure of being able to prepare the article you request."[87]

As Presbyterian women gradually developed their own internal network of contacts and supporters, a comparable network evolved among social activists. Although such networking is well known within the business world, it has not been studied carefully in the church. Because Social Gospel advocates within the PCUS were a deeply committed minority, they sought each other's company and advice. The Atlanta circle related to W. L. Lingle provides an excellent example. The Reverend Dunbar H. Ogden pastored Central Presbyterian Church across the street from Georgia's capitol. He was not only a personal friend of Lingle's, but the two were equally committed to the social ministry of the Presbyterian church. In 1913 he shared with Lingle his opinion of a new book entitled *Christ in the Social Order*. The book was orthodox from the standpoint of the PCUS, challenging individual members to involvement but not the church. Ogden was disappointed in the author who "lacked the fire that I wish linked with conservatism." The book was "too largely a defense of the present order." When a staff member left his church a few years later, Ogden wrote Lingle asking for a young seminarian who could reach the boarding houses and apartments near his church: "In working out this down town problem there will be a large amount of ministry to the poor, and the man who takes the work must have sympathy toward this class and wisdom in helping them practically. This feature of the work will also mean close co-operation with other Christian forces in the working out of our city wide problems." The person would also be responsible for a new ministry to inner-city blacks. Lingle often used Ogden at Montreat conferences to help liberate the PCUS "from the death grip of reactionaries." In 1915 Ogden wrote his friend that he had been invited to deliver two series of addresses in Birmingham and planned one topic on "The Social Message of the Bible": "You see how you have been leading me out. I trust that your platform has not been tainted past fumigation." Lingle recommended Ogden as Professor of Church History at Union Seminary, but the idea did not appeal to his Atlanta friend: "I would enjoy the life, but I feel a desire to be in the very thick of the fight while the strength of young manhood is mine." But later, in his senior years, he might enjoy the challenge of delivering lectures "on the Social message of the Bible. . . ."[88]

Ogden's most famous parishioner at Central Presbyterian was another friend of Lingle's, John J. Eagan. Born in Griffin, Georgia, Eagan inherited money and began a distinguished business career in Atlanta. A devoted churchman, he served as superintendent of the Sabbath School at Central Presbyterian for twenty years, as an elder, and a member of the Home Mission Board. He contributed generously to mountain schools, served as chairman of the subcommittee on mountain work, chairman of the board of Berry Schools, and began Rabun Gap-Nacoochee School in north Georgia. He provided books, especially on social ministries, for Union Seminary, and engaged in the private charities expected of such philanthropists. In his application of the gospel to society he was as cautious as Ogden and Lingle. Although he read widely in the new sociological literature, he was unsatisfied by its exclusive emphasis upon changing society. Nor did socialism appeal to him: "The tendency of modern socialism is to exalt 'Thou shalt love thy neighbor as thyself' above the first and great commandment," causing many people to serve humanity as their only effort to love God.[89]

But during the second decade of the century he also became deeply committed to social justice. He read widely on "the Negro problem" and sought racial cooperation. The works of Social Gospel advocate Josiah Strong particularly influenced him. Although he wished the term "sociology" could be replaced by "Christianity," that would be possible only when the church assumed its social obligations. "I am convinced that a careful study of the life of Christ will convince one that He was tremendously concerned about the bodies as well as the souls of men," he wrote Lingle. "You know better than I the proportion of His ministry that was devoted to healing the sick, feeding the hungry and ministering to the broken hearted." He rejoiced when Lingle left Atlanta for the seminary because he believed seminaries devoted too little attention to practical work. Applied Christianity should rank equal in the curriculum to systematic theology, and he believed that Union Seminary students should spend more time among the needy people of Richmond.[90]

Eagan certainly practiced in Atlanta what he preached to Richmond. He became an active member of an interdenominational Social Gospel group, the Men and Religion Forward Movement. Atlanta was one of ninety cities where the group organized a chapter and Eagan was elected president at its first meeting. The first task of the organization was a successful campaign against prostitution. Next came the purchase of a home for unwed mothers, prison reform, prohibition, support of child labor legislation, and economic justice for workers. The organization became involved with organized labor in 1913 when it supported a strike by the Typographical Union against a Baptist publishing house. Months later laborers at the Fulton Bag and Cotton Mills in Cabbagetown, a poor white community in southeast Atlanta, organized a union. The company promptly fired seventy-eight union members, and the Men and Religion Forward Movement again supported the workers. The group's executive committee published a weekly bulletin in the *Atlanta Constitution* to state their view of social issues and injustice. The movement also helped organize public meetings to publicize the wretched mill conditions that led to unionization. *The Journal of Labor* expressed gratitude to John Eagan and ministers who spoke at labor rallies and so loyally supported workers. Eagan as president of the group addressed one of the mass meetings where he talked of the necessity of applying Christian principles to the solution of labor problems. The Men and Religion Forward Movement also endorsed labor legislation pending in the state legislature. A historian has called the Atlanta group's involvement with labor justice one of the major deviations from individualistic southern religion and John Eagan the primary architect of that policy. Perhaps it was not coincidental that during the labor disputes Eagan was reading Walter Rauschenbusch's book, *Thrice Born Men*.[91]

Eagan continued both his active public involvement in the Social Gospel and his private commitment to social justice. In 1919 he was elected first president of the Council on Interracial Cooperation, which he helped found. Two years later in 1921 he turned over his enormously profitable American Cast Iron Pipe Company to its employees. His outline for the corporation's management was simple but radical: a reasonable living wage must be paid to the lowest paid workman; constant employment must be provided every employee; the Golden Rule must govern all relations between employer and employee. Management-labor relations were coordinated by a Board of Operatives elected annually from among workers by their peers.[92] In a sense the reorganization of the company into a venture of cooperative capitalism was the culmination of his long Social Gospel pilgrimage.

Lingle's network of allies stretched beyond Atlanta and involved many of his former students. Of the hundreds who owed him gratitude for their theology and social consciousness, none was more intriguing than Witherspoon Dodge. Just out of seminary in 1913 Dodge became pastor of Central Presbyterian Church in Anderson, South Carolina. He considered Lingle the formative influence in his seminary career and maintained contact through the years. Unlike Eagan, Ogden, and Lingle, Dodge fits the model of a revolutionary advocate of the Social Gospel. He frequently clashed with church elders because of his unorthodox theology and reform minded sermons. He considered even Lingle to be too cautious and conservative. After volunteering to write articles for the *Union Seminary Review* to balance the journal's "reactionary views," he declined to do so because he was too busy fighting for "civic and social righteousness" and because his article would be "so full of Christianity and so lacking in traditional theology" that it would never be allowed into print anyway.[93]

Perhaps he was correct. The activities of Lingle, Ogden, Eagan, Dodge, Winsborough, and others were not warmly received in many church quarters. The major Presbyterian forum for those who opposed the Social Gospel was the *Presbyterian Standard*. It seldom deviated from Old School Presbyterianism and the doctrine of the spirituality of the church. The editors attacked "social service," the term used by Social Gospel advocates within the PCUS, because it ignored saving souls in order to minister to slums, factory districts, and "submerged classes." The editors did not object to better wages or shorter hours, old age pensions, or other reforms. But social service had a vision limited to the present and trusted too much in civil legislation. Their advice was to transform society by saving souls: "Make the tree good, and the fruit cannot be evil. Convert Zaccheus, and he will restore fourfold for all that he has gained by extortion. Is not this the one all-inclusive mission of the Church?"[94] The paper was loyal to that creed throughout the decade. It denounced aggressive women and opposed woman suffrage. When Walter Rauschenbusch died Lingle wept; but the *Standard*'s editor thought the theologian's conception of Christianity shallow, his influence and teachings "far from wholesome." In 1913 coeditor R. C. Reed condemned sociology and socialism, prompting Lingle to respond that Reed did not understand the difference between the two. Reed conceded his ignorance but did not change his mind. That began a long and testy correspondence. When Lingle demanded that the PCUS denounce lynching, Reed responded that the church "should not go into politics in order to secure social and political reforms." Lingle wrote Reed denouncing the tendency within the PCUS to ignore "current evils" and praised the tendency of "the Church at large" "to seek *social, industrial,* and *political* reforms through means of civil legislation." Reed responded that Jesus had not agitated for social or political reforms, to which Lingle replied that Jesus certainly did teach ethical principles "which cut right at the heart of the social evils of the day," and James "spoke out against those who did not pay a sufficient wage."[95]

Reed was not convinced. In 1918 he praised a pamphlet entitled "The Social Ministry of the Church to Those Outside of Its Membership" for its sound theology. Containing essays written primarily by members of the PCUS, the pamphlet affirmed the exclusively spiritual character of the church. One of the essayists, Dr. W. Irving Carroll, had "hit the nail most squarely on the head" when he wrote: "As to the social mission of the Church to those outside of its membership, may I simply say that it has none! None, absolutely none. Its one work is the . . . salvation, not the education, nor the civilization, nor the social uplift, of lost sinners." Reed agreed: "This is the doctrine that needs to be proclaimed upon the housetop, and written in golden letters over the doors of all our church buildings." What was needed, he added later, was "Old Time Religion," not the "uplift of human-ity." Although the paper did not advise neglecting the poor, it did deplore the church's neglect of the rich: "The influence of the rich for good or evil is so much greater than that of the poor that the church should feel deeply concerned to enlist them for Christ."[96]

Conservative editors were by no means the only critics of the Social Gospel. When a prominent Presbyterian in Alabama wrote the history of the PCUS in his state, he devoted special attention to the failure of settlement house ministries among Italian steel workers, which he blamed on too much Social Gospel influence and too little Bible study and evangelism.[97]

Virtually all of the animosities, disagreements, and ideological divisions within the PCUS focused finally on one issue, ecumen-ism. Conservatives blamed interdenominational groups for dilut-ing Calvinist doctrine and fostering heresy. The first round in the decade long debate began in 1908 with the organization of the Federal Council of Churches of Christ in America. The council became involved in all aspects of social ministries including child labor, labor-management conflict, trusts, prohibition, divorce, and international arbitration. Such involvements ran counter to the doctrine of the spirituality of the church. The PCUS joined the Federal Council, provoking furious criticism and causing the General Assembly to vote to withdraw in 1911. But the Assembly reversed its actions and reaffiliated in 1912. Despite annual de-bates and bitter conservative opposition to the affiliation, moder-ate leaders managed to defeat their attempts to withdraw from the Federal Council until 1931.[98]

The council's critics directed their fire at its Social Gospel proclivities. They attacked its leaders, such as University of Chicago professor Shailer Mathews, and its programs. During the 1912 General Assembly debate on reentering the council, the Reverend R. C. Reed, coeditor of the *Presbyterian Standard*, opposed reaffiliation because the council "meddled with political matters, which we opposed as a Church." In 1914 a number of presbyteries urged the PCUS to withdraw. Their petition was defeated but not before the newly created Committee on the Relation of Christian Faith and Social Service was instructed to inform the council that the General Assembly did not approve of its Social Service programs. The mood in 1915 was better. The General Assembly congratulated the council on its efforts to help country churches, improve rural life, and strengthen the family. But the Assembly again denounced its involvement with secular matters extraneous to the mission of the church.[99]

The Federal Council had its defenders within the PCUS, especially W. L. Lingle. In 1913 he served on one of the council's commissions, and through him council defenders tried to counter opposition within the church. A Greensboro attorney urged Lingle to use his considerable influence to educate Presbyterians by writing articles explaining the council's work. Lingle moved quickly to do so using literature furnished by the council. The secretary of the Federal Council denied that it deemphasized "the spiritual background of social reconstruction," and urged Lingle to emphasize that point in his articles. Dr. J. R. Howerton, whose book on the Social Gospel influenced so many Presbyterians, also used his influence to quiet critics and served a term as the council's president.[100]

As fiercely as the two sides contested this issue, the Interchurch World Movement created even greater furor. Lingle once again stood at center stage in the controversy. In 1920 he addressed a conference of the Interchurch World Movement in Richmond. His topic, "Christianizing The Industrial Order," reflected the Social Gospel direction of the organization and so impressed some Methodist and Episcopalian delegates that they invited him to give the same address in their community. Conservatives opposed the new organization, conceding its noble objectives but fearing that it would seek uniformity, "minimize creed," and "shock our ideas of the sphere of the Church."[101] Concern about the General Assembly's position caused both advocates and opponents to bombard Presbyterian papers with articles.

But before the 1920 General Assembly met, another issue loomed even larger. For those supporting ecumenism, the logical first step was to heal the historic breach between the two wings of America's Presbyterian church, the PCUS and the PCUSA. W. L. Lingle vacillated on the question, favoring unification early in the century, opposing it in 1911, and equivocating in 1918. He devoted the January, 1918, issue of the *Union Seminary Review* to a series of position papers on the subject. The General Assembly in 1917 had appointed a committee to study the possibility of federation, but the PCUS was deeply divided. Some authors favored organic union of all Presbyterian churches, others wanted a federation that left each intact, and some opposed all forms of merger. Those who favored organic union also tended to be the ones most sympathetic to social service.[102]

Debate on the issue swirled across the pages of Presbyterian papers for two years. Although Lingle did not favor merger until a clear consensus supported it within the PCUS, he did defened organic union in theory. He wrote that he had "never been able to see any great principle of the Gospel or Presbyterianism separating the Presbyterian Churches of America. . . ." When a minister disagreed with this advice because the PCUSA made pronouncements on political and social issues, Lingle retorted that even southern Presbyterians spoke on such issues, especially on temperance. His antagonist admitted that the PCUS did occasionally violate its own principles by passing resolutions on social questions, but insisted that the PCUSA did so much more frequently. Thorton Whaling, professor at Columbia Seminary in South Carolina, led the campaign against Lingle. Although Whaling accepted cooperation between the two bodies, he vigorously opposed organic union. The debate intensified in 1919 when the First Presbyterian Church of Louisville, Kentucky, voted to join the PCUSA. At the 1919 General Assembly, many synods and presbyteries denounced the union movement. But advocates, including Lingle's longtime friend Dunbar Ogden of Atlanta, urged union talks between the two churches.[103] The debate became increasingly nasty in 1919 with acrimonious personal correspondence and an allegation by Ogden that Thornton Whaling "was after" him at the meeting of his presbytery. The newspaper debate became so intense that editors suggested it cease.[104]

As the decade closed the issues unleashed by twenty years of conflict came together at the 1920 General Assembly. Opponents of Presbyterian union and the Interchurch World Movement mobilized all their resources against Social Gospel ecumenism. The first decision faced by the Assembly provided delegates a clear choice. Five men were nominated as presiding officer, among them seminary professors Walter Lingle and Thornton Whaling. Four roll calls and three hours later, delegates elected Lingle moderator. Later a majority report favoring participation in the Interchurch World Movement won 136 to 103 over a minority report proposing that the PCUS withdraw. Lingle as moderator then refused to vote on a tie when conservatives requested that a questionnaire on membership in the group be sent to all PCUS congregations. By not voting, Lingle defeated the proposal. His friend John Eagan congratulated him on keeping the PCUS in the Interchurch World Movement. He believed that the united movement of the church even with its imperfections was better than sectarian competition. Lingle savored his victory, aware that the real issue had been his theology and the issues he had championed for a decade:

> When I was nominated as Moderator, I felt that the Assembly was face to face with the question as to whether the general position that I took in my articles was correct, or whether the position of my leading critic, who was also nominated, was also correct; in fact, when I was nominated without any seeking on my part, and without my knowledge, I just asked the Lord to show me in that election whether I had been right or wrong.

Somehow I feel that the election was His answer to that question. . . . Perhaps I put the wrong interpretation on all of this, but somehow I feel that it is the Lord's answer to my challenge to the Church to cultivate the spirit of love and unity and fellowship with the other great Presbyterian bodies of this country.[105]

Thus vindicated in his own mind, Lingle expanded his vision within an increasingly conservative church. He followed the Sprunt Lectures in 1929 with a series of hard-hitting Social Gospel sermons in the 1930s and advocacy of desegregation in the 1940s and 1950s. John Eagan continued with his interracial work and his collectivization of American Cast Iron Pipe until his death in 1924. Witherspoon Dodge despaired of ever reforming Presbyterians, became a Congregational minister in Atlanta during the 1920s and a CIO organizer in the 1930s when he was nearly stoned to death by an antiunion mob at Gaffney, South Carolina.[106] The PCUS withdrew from the Federal Council of Churches in 1931, resisted desegregation, and was able to reunite with its northern wing only in 1983 when many conservative congregations withdrew to join the Presbyterian Church in America. Many Social Gospel dreams from those early years died in subsequent decades. But it was a goodly fight they made and a bright fire they kindled.

Religion and Politics in The South

SAMUEL S. HILL

The interaction of religion and politics in the South is a subject that has attained a fresh prominence recently. The campaign and election of Jimmy Carter in 1976 converted a hitherto charming and somewhat eccentric phrase, "born-again Christian," into a national issue. The personal faith of the Sunday School-teaching Southern Baptist from Plains, Georgia, became an item of concern for a sizeable sector of the national electorate. They feared that an evangelical Christian might use the presidency to promote one religious perspective—as Roman Catholic John Kennedy had not done between 1961 and 1963. Southerners may or may not have favored Mr. Carter, but they knew better than to fear a religion-inspired misuse of the powers of the nation's highest office.

Beginning in 1976 and especially since 1979, the religious issue has gained a general American notoriety. A passionate cause to restore the nation to its senses and its divine mission for a small minority, it is the occasion for deep concern, sometimes fear, to a somewhat larger minority. Most Americans are ranged in between, hearing appeals for their votes and sorting out their loyalties. This includes most southerners too.

Notwithstanding its reputation as a bastion of evangelical strength, the region is far from being a "solid South" on the side of the "New Christian Right" (NCR). It is not even the soil from which that religious-political movement grew. Conservative leaders such as Howard Phillips, Paul Weyrich, and Richard Viguerie approached Jerry Falwell, Pat Robertson, and Jim Bakker in 1978 about forging an alliance. Its design was to bring together the moral and political program of the former with the particular evangelicalism of the latter. NCR support was sought also because it stressed a specific morality and a vigorous patriotism.

Support for the Moral Majority, Inc., the Falwell-led organization and the most visible of the religious-political organizations, is not concentrated in the South. He is a southern pastor, but of an independent Baptist congregation. He has enlisted a following that attracts numbers of upper South people but few from the deep South. Moreover the rallies he leads and the supporters he attracts are as likely to be associated with the Middle West as with the South. Indeed this cadre of Christian soldiers cannot be identified as regional; they come mostly from a diagonal swath that extends from the Middle Atlantic coast along the line of "border states" to southern California.

Still, there are other clues that the South is home base for the new religious-political cause in America. Jim Bakker's rather independent but similar campaign for a Christianized land is conducted from Charlotte. (He is from Michigan.) Similarly, Charles Stanley's campaign from Atlanta, James Robison's from Fort Worth, and Jimmy Swaggart's from Baton Rouge—all three are southerners themselves and have primarily regional audiences. Having a greater national appeal is Pat Robertson, a Virginian, whose sophistication in the application of Christian teachings to public affairs may make his the most effectual enterprise in the long run.

Clearly, the South is playing a role in the cause that aims to ground the political direction of the country in a moral understanding having its source in the Bible. From its population are coming a few highly visible leaders and a considerable following. Southerners are often responsive to the moral agenda advanced by the Moral Majority, Christian Voice, Religious Roundtable, the National Christian Political Action Committee, and other right-wing groups.[1] Most of the items on this agenda have to do with "traditional values," in particular, family and gender ethics. The most prominent are opposition to abortion, pornography, homosexuality, and the Equal Rights Amendment. One of these, the anti-abortion movement, has not previously been a traditional moral concern, at least in a public way, in the South. In the context of regional ethics, it is likely to be tied in with condemnation of sexual activity before and outside marriage. Recent research discloses that southern blacks, too, score very high on support for traditional family values. Opposition to abortion is strong. There is significant opposition to birth control and lack of tolerance for homosexuals.[2]

Conspicuous by its low standing on the NCR's list is the use of alcoholic beverages. The anti alcohol cause, long a staple of regional proscriptions, is receiving little attention from the NCR Instead, what is seen to be eating at the vitals of America relates mostly to the family but with the public schools and federal government policies also of concern. Individualistic morality—what used to be called the "finger sins"—appears to have minor importance. However, in the churches and counties and towns of the South, the manufacture, sale, and consumption of alcoholic beverages remains a central moral issue.

The emergence of the New Christian Right on the southern scene thus indicates discontinuity as well as continuity relative to the South's past. For one thing, some issues that have not been high on the southern morality list are now at least mentioned. One is abortion, another is homosexuality. These probably have been items of importance to many people all along, but they have been brought into the arena of public debate rather recently.

At another level, some issues that have been central in the South's moral understanding are not a part of the NCR program. The two central ones are the use of alcoholic beverages, as noted, and the racial ethic, the latter no longer a stated issue in southern churches and not at all an issue in the New Christian Right movement. Surprising to many outsiders is that this fundamentalist movement does not preach (or knowingly practice) racism. Although the ideology and style of the movement do not make it attractive to very many black people, and although racial justice is not a priority item on the NCR list, blacks are welcomed and not discriminated against. The traditional southern (white) convictions about the separation of black people and white people and about blacks' divinely-ordained inferiority are no part of this group's ethical teachings.

A third indicator of discontinuity on the recent scene is the influence of leadership that is not part of the historic southern mainstream. In fact much of it is orchestrated through moral-political agents and agencies based ouside the region, NCPAC, Christian Voice, and the like, and it is highly organized. In Michael Lienesch's words: "The New Christian Right is far from the model of the irrational mass movement."[3] It is constituted mostly of members of independent churches (Baptist and other) and of quite conservative segments of the regional mainline denominations, the Southern Baptist most notably.[4] Lienesch has found it to be "an alliance of conservative preachers," something of an "elite phenomenon," "a small group of preachers and politicians allied to the right wing of the Republican party."[5] One wonders when last a moral crusade had strength in the American South without either being a long-standing regional consensus or having endorsement by the major religious bodies.

A glance at the history of southern religious-political enterprises will serve to point out the established traditions in relation to which recent developments are continuous or discontinuous. First, one must recall that there have been many such movements, covering a wide span of concerns. They range from the Southern Christian Tenant Farmers' Union on the left to the Ku Klux Klan on the right. They further include the various Prohibitionist organizations, the Coalition for Better Television, voter registration drives, the Southern Christian Leadership Conference, the Fellowship of Southern Churchmen, the Commission on Interracial Cooperation, the Association of Southern Women for the Prevention of Lynching, and many more. Southern church women, notably, have conducted numerous moral campaigns. They have organized to improve the conditions of people in prison, the poor, immigrants, industrial workers, and blacks in slavery and under segregation; also to eradicate the discrimination of women and the ravages of alcohol abuse as well as lynching.[6]

These do not, totalled, add up to a specifiable Social Gospel tradition. The South has never produced a major movement making general impact and attracting a large following to compare with the Social Gospel movement in northern Protestantism between 1890 and 1930. Nevertheless, Social Gospel impulses have appeared continually from the Old South period straight through to the present.[7] They have cropped up among blacks, whites, and blacks and whites together; in deep South states and border states alike; in both rural and urban areas; through church bodies and through *ad hoc* agencies; and from several denominations. It could hardly have been otherwise, given the heavy stress evangelical Christianity has placed on righteousness, love of neighbor, disciplined behavior, and a sensitive conscience.[8] For all its shortcomings, southern ethical sensitivity has been keen, not repressible for long. In fact, even in the area of greatest blindness, whites' religious justification of slavery and segregation, much soul-searching has occurred, issuing sometimes in guilt and defensiveness, frequently also in deeds of mercy.

At least four main types of religious-political activism have been common in southern life: 1) direct and intentional; 2) indirect and consequential; 3) oblique; and 4) personal influence as a social ethic.

1. Direct and intentional forms are the most apparent and, doubtless the most numerous. They are brought into being by people who discern a need, who have a concern that calls for concrete expression. In the era of the Great Depression a small band of southern Protestant ministers, concerned with the severe poverty they saw around them, organized the Fellowship of Southern Churchmen to work for a more economically just society. Heavily influenced by Reinhold Niebuhr, they thought and taught, they lobbied and organized in and on behalf of the church. They regarded their vision of a new, more just society

as one envisioned by Christ and manifesting his compassion for the poor, the powerless, and those confined to caste and ghetto among southern whites and blacks alike. Always a small group and far too oriented toward change for the vast majority of southerners, they made little impact. But they were a prophetic voice, purveyors of an alternate societal style, a witness against and for. The FOC was unmistakably southern, founded and carried on by southerners, its goals directed to the specific contours of regional life.[9]

Related in intention, more focused in aim, and with a higher proportion of black members was the Southern Tenant Farmers' Union founded in 1934. Reaching its heights in 1935 and 1936, it was effective for less than a decade. Its efforts to realign southern economic and racial patterns in a time of great deprivation cut across the grain, called into question, and irritated. Although seeming alien to most, it too was indigenous. From a number of perspectives, what could have been more southern than the congeries of sharecroppers, farmers, the poor, black and white field hands, and good Christians yearning to do the Lord's will through building the Kingdom of God?[10]

The Southern Christian Leadership Conference is a third example of the "direct and intentional" type of religious-political movement in the South. Led by Martin Luther King, Jr., and other ministers, it was an organization of black Christians who sought the embodiment of the teachings of Jesus in the laws of American society. There is historical irony in that this, the most effective religious-political organization in southern history, was black in origin, achievement, and (largely) membership; its work changed the face of the entire American society, not alone the South.

2. The "indirect and consequential" type of movement has long been present in the South but by its very nature is difficult to identify. This term refers to forces in society that reflect the impact of the values the churches stand for without rationalized activities toward the achievement of those goals.[11]

An example of this type of movement is the effect of the evangelical denominations on the society of late colonial Virginia. Largely an extension of English society, Virginia installed an established church and practiced a consensus about class hierarchy. In the first case, the chaotic implications of tolerating religious diversity had to be prevented. In the second, clear thinking and social realism indicated that society's being made up of social classes, hierarchically ordered, is a good thing and best for all. In the nature of things, some are above others; some are owners, others are workers; some are free people, others are slaves; and so on.

This social philosophy was challenged and largely overturned between 1740 and 1790.[12] A policy of religious liberty replaced establishmentarianism. Personal achievement supplanted wealth, primogeniture, recognition by family name, and other feudalistic values as the agents for conferring identity. Methodist and Baptist preachments contributed significantly to this revolution in social attitudes. Faith claimed for one's self and church membership personally chosen stood in a reciprocal relation with democratic values in the public realm. Evangelical faith accomplished more than it intended; it helped produce a new understanding of political life.

3. The "oblique" relation between religion and politics is always unusual but almost always dramatic. In cases of this sort, indigenous Christian activities grow from the cultural soil sideways, so to speak, in order to stand for something, to make a witness. They are by definition radical. To their proponents they are "radical" according to the Latin root, to the root (or "radish") of something. They seek to be radically obedient to Christian teachings and are regularly out of step with cultural mores and conventions. In the eyes of the society, thus, they seem strange, even weird, possibly subversive. A quality of theirs that is especially irritating to the society at large is the absence of a goal orientation. They do not set out to *do* very much, instead pray to *be* very much. As they can be drawn out to say, their calling is to be faithful, not to be successful.

Will Campbell of the Committee of Southern Churchmen and Clarence Jordan of Koinonia Farm, in their quite different and unique ways, have made a real if oblique impact on the South. Neither has sought to revolutionize the public order, neither has structured a program for changing laws or electing new kinds of people to office. In fact neither has even made organized efforts to publicize its own existence. But the Koinonia Partners seek to provide an alternative to a consumerist life-style and to incarnate reconciliation between races, classes, and genders. Will Campbell and his committee offer themselves as apostles to the Ku Klux Klan, rednecks, and prisoners on death row. Both would like to see the world changed. Out of faithfulness they offer their visions of the Kingdom of God in the hope that their God, as he wills, will bring the genuine vision into being.

4. A final type of religious-political activism is personal influence. Perhaps this form seems strange to all but evangelical perspectives but there it is natural and central. This is particularly true where the Puritan spirit remains strong and revivalism is the dominant school of that approach to Protestantism, as in the American South. And when in the South this is further blended with a Gemeinschaft theory of society, the power of the position is great. "Personal influence" notions rely heavily on the impact one person makes on another—and, presumably, on a whole society when enough "anothers" have witnessed the right way. On this view, a central aspect of Christian responsibility is setting the right example. One ascertains what are the rights and the wrongs, in specific actions and in attitudes, and behaves accordingly. Being morally serious in that way is simply a Christian's duty; no other incentive is needed. Yet, the southern faithful live in a culture where neighborliness, more broadly, awareness of others and their well-being, is a premium virtue. Therefore (more than in most cultural settings) southern Christians reckon their duty in terms of doing right so that others may observe and follow in the correct path. This includes the evangelistic hope that, by seeing a Christian's spirit and moral rectitude, a lost person may be swayed to following Christ.

This "personal influence" theory of public responsibility lives on in the South and functions as many Christians' deepest understanding of their calling. Whatever its strengths, this position attaches little significance to the structures of society, such as economic, political, and racial. It therefore fails to touch some public issues and processes. The relation of this southern "personal influence" ethic to the New Christian Right is ambivalent. Procedurally they differ; one organizes for action, the other awaits its impact. As far as moral positions are concerned, they concur at a number of points.

Several references have been made to the South's black Christians in this treatment of religion and politics in the South. The patterns of their behavior sometimes fit those of whites' behavior, as has been seen. But sometimes they do not. This singularity of black religious-political behavior is utterly predictable, of course, in line with the distinctiveness of black culture generally and black evangelical religion specifically. Two additional features of black Christian ethics will serve to make the point. First, in the words of Perkins, Fairchild, and Havens, "the racial experience, not the religious experience, appears to be dominant for blacks." They infer from survey research data that "if anything, the religion of blacks may reinforce their political beliefs and behavior."[13] Thus, blacks are not highly responsive to "morality-based appeals" for support of particular candidates and causes. Second, the juxtaposition of "liberal" and "conservative" positions on different ethical issues is unique to the black community. On "law and order" issues and on economic questions, blacks are typically "liberal." But on matters of traditional family morality they are regularly "conservative."[14] The passion to eliminate racial inequalities is predominant in the ethics of southern blacks, but the commitment to home and family is vigorous.

This glance at the major conceptions of how religion and politics are related highlight the distinctive course of southern religious history. All continue to be a part of southern understanding as they have been for a long time. A specific tradition exists, the South's own. It is a "limited distinctiveness," in Carl Degler's term, inasmuch as it shares some perspectives present among Christians at other times and places, and in some respects it rearranges older approaches. It is not to be classified as radical sectarianism in either the fundamentalist sense of being suspicious toward culture or with respect to the social philosophy of the Mennonite and Amish people descended from the sixteenth–century Anabaptist movement. But the South's religious-political understanding is not a great deal nearer to Luther and Calvin than to the Anabaptists' theory of separation and the shunning of public affairs and institutions. It is the South's singular tradition. It derives more from revivalistic Protestantism, its theology and methods, than from any rationalized interpretation of the proper relationship between church and state. In certain respects, it reflects its descent from Calvinism, notably in its conviction that religion and politics (church and state) are partners in creating and maintaining a godly society. However, it veers from that path and strikes its own course in seeing the role of religion in the political sphere as more indirect and epiphenomenal. In its heart of hearts, southern religion puts its faith in the personal piety of converted individuals whose lives reflect biblical righteousness in daily behavior.

That summation of the deepest layer of the southern religious attitude toward "religion and politics" tells a great deal. On the side of what it does not mean, this is not classic conservatism as seen, for example, in the Republican party. The mood is not "the less government, the better" nor is it "remove government from public affairs so that the private sector can do its work." Thus, the political spirit of the "typical Midwestern Republican farmer" is not duplicated by mainstream southerners. As a matter of fact, recent research discloses that "southerners have more rather than less confidence in the federal government than the rest of the nation," a finding contrary to the expectations of the political scientist who conducted that survey.[15]

Southern political concern has not sought to lessen the role of government, rather to place the right quality of people in office. Before the 1960s, much attention concentrated on the racial issue—and earlier on upholding other regional cultural traditions as well. Some resistance to black people persists in one of the "three Souths" (the "traditional," the "new," and the "black") identified by Michael Mezey. In the "traditional" segment, made up of whites mostly of low status and from rural areas, he found a higher percentage intolerant of deviant groups, conservative on women's rights, and committed to orthodox religious and moral positions.[16] Overall, the concern of southern voters has shifted away from specifically regional issues. Instead voters look for "good people," "the right man," candidates with integrity—and, like voters everywhere, with personal winsomeness and credibility.

It should not be surprising, then, that Jimmy Carter carried the South in 1976. In addition to being a son of the region—the only presidential candidate in a long time who did not speak with an accent—he was a virtuous man. Southern voters prefer candidates who radiate personal piety and openly confess a Christian commitment. Nevertheless, southern white evangelicals gave Gerald Ford a strong majority (59.2 percent). White non-evangelicals gave Carter a slight edge (51.9 percent). Black southerners supported Carter overwhelmingly (92 percent).[17]

The complexity of southern evangelical voting behavior was evident in 1976. Carter's disappointing foreign policy, climaxed by the Iranian hostage crisis, together with other features of his administration, gave the 1980 election the appearance of a plebiscite on that administration—though more for the rest of the nation than for the South.[18] The complexity actually heightened in 1980. The orthodox within the southern Christian population did not present a "behavioral uniformity." Carter seems to have fared "rather better among southern white Protestants than recent Democratic candidates."[19] This conclusion is attributable, most likely, to Democratic party support and to his personal piety. Carter's strength lay partly in his personal religiosity. But that was proven to be no longer enough. Furthermore he was preempted on the South's own grounds, its strong feelings about moral and social issues, by Ronald Reagan, a much less pious man who embodied a religious-patriotic sense and who lent his support to the denunciation of the right sins and promoted traditional values for the family and the public schools.

The "Solid South" has not existed since the New Deal era as far as voting patterns are concerned. But 1976 and, especially, 1980 may signal a more significant watershed in southern political behavior than 1948. The interjection of new kinds of moral and social issues and the fading of regional conventions and personal loyalties into a recessive position mark a dramatic change.

Southerners' commitment to "good people" and "righteous living" then does play a part in such appeal as the organized New
Christian Right began to have in 1979 and 1980. As the Moral
Majority, Inc., and various national political organizations spread
their message through massive direct mail campaigns and
numerous television programs, they touched some southern sensitivity.[20] Some moral causes that southerners had not gotten very
excited about, such as abortion and homosexuality, acquired importance. The issue of prayer in the public schools also gained
some following. (That issue was especially troublesome for many
Southern Baptists who saw the hallowed principle of separation
of church and state as suggesting support for the 1962 Supreme
Court decision.) On the societal level, the NCR's notions of the
nature and role of America fit rather neatly with several traditional southern positions. Regard for this nation as a land of
"chosen people," or at least as imbued with a mission to the
whole world, belongs to the southern religious—and social—
outlook.[21] A certain regional militancy, at worst the South's high
incidence of violence and at best its willingness to defend the
native land, played into the New Right's program of military
preparedness against a malevolent and aggressive foreign enemy.

The appeal of the New Christian Right is something of an
anomaly. Southern evangelicals and others are responsive to it,
often finding it wholesome and consistent with their traditional
views. They also recognize that it sounds a little different from
what they are accustomed to hearing. Its platforms, its proponents, and its strategies are mildly foreign to regional conventions. This was dramatically true of the 1984 reelection campaign
of Senator Jesse Helms, the incumbent North Carolina Republican, whose case is sufficiently important to warrant direct attention. Helms's popularity sheds a great deal of light on the religious-political trends in the recent South.

It is striking that Helms's position is primarily ideological, not
moral, and pertains to economics first, then to politics. This fact
must be placed alongside the research findings that southern

evangelical public concerns are with moral issues rather than economic or political ones. Corwin Smidt has found that "only a minority of southern white Evangelicals are, by nature, across-the-board political conservatives." More pointedly, they "tend to be cultural conservatives, particularly when issues involve traditional moral values."²² The attitudes of southerners generally are illuminated by comparing them with the rest of the nation. Baker, Steed, and Moreland suggest that in southern states and communities "issues such as abortion, pornography, school prayer, gambling, and legalization of liquor . . . occupy the center ring of political discourse." In contrast, on the national level "it appears unlikely that . . . moral issues will supplant economic, military, or foreign policy issues as topics of dominant concern."²³

Southern political behavior reflects the Gemeinschaft theory of society. Localism, for so long a regional value, persists. And life is still understood to consist of personal relationships responsibly conducted according to the canons of personal morality. "The home, the school, and the church" and "good Christians in office" are concepts that have staying power.

Against this background, the case of Jesse Helms is illuminating. In a traditionally Democratic state with a huge proportion of evangelicals, his popularity is amazingly strong. For one thing, he is a "man of principle." (Others describe him as "stubborn" or as one whose disrespect for other points of view renders him unwilling to negotiate.) Southerners admire that kind of person. Many of them believe the Helms campaign ads that describe his opponent as a "wishy-washy politician." Secondly, he takes a firm stand on moral issues, the NCR's list—the use of tobacco and liquor is missing. And third, he divides the world into good and evil, on political, military, and economic topics as well as on moral ones.

Helms successfully appeals to people whose first love is morality when his primary commitment is ideological. What animates Helms is his unwavering conviction about free enterprise economics. He is evangelistic in his belief that that aspect of human

affairs is guided by an "invisible hand" (in the language of Adam
Smith). He is simply lucky that he also espouses, until recently in
quite a secondary way, the morality of the NCR and that that
agenda, in turn, is similar to traditional southern morality. To
reiterate: Helms's political popularity is due to the sheer good
fortune of his being conservative on both economic-political issues and on moral issues. What ranks highest with him has rated
comparatively low for many of his supporters. But they are at-
tuned to conservatism and, notably, to the crusade-style preachments he uses to convey his message. Social-political and moral
matters alike have the ring of an uncompromising divine righteousness when declaimed by Senator Helms. He and his supporters take great glee in the moralistic cadences with which he
(like Israel's God of old) routs the enemies of righteousness. He
has put together the right "package" for assuring political success
in North Carolina. And evidence suggests that he embodies that
dual conservatism in a quite natural way, rather than his adding
the moral platform simply in order to win votes.

Two features on the southern political landscape bring into
relief Helms's surprising popularity.

1. Evangelicals as a whole find their "relationship with the
secular Right to be rather frustrating," notwithstanding their
common support for several candidates in 1980.[24] This is partly
because evangelicals are primarily concerned with certain social issues, while secular conservatives are primarily concerned with economic issues. For most of his career, Jesse
Helms has been identified with the agenda of the "secular
conservatives." The addition of the moral list, although sin-
cere, has come rather recently. To put this point in perspective, one should ask whether conservatives such as Barry Gold-
water or Jack Kemp or Robert Taft would generate much of a
following in the South. It is unlikely—although the number of
outspoken, issue-minded economic conservatives is growing in
the South as the managerial sector expands.

2. In two of the three Souths (to refer again to Mezey's
construction), economic liberalism continues to show strength.
In the "traditional South" (whites of low status, mostly rural), a

measure of economic liberalism persists. Social services, welfare provisions, and government involvement enjoy some popularity there. In the "black South," a quite liberal economic philosophy prevails. Working through the structures of society and benefitting from the effect of changed laws has inclined the region's blacks to prefer a more centralized and regulated economic system.[25]

Where are we now in the relations between religion and politics in the South? The question is more intriguing and important than it is answerable. Certainly the situation is too complex to admit of much predicting. One factor to trace is the power of the black population. At present, black political power is comparatively small, and coalescing black and white political concerns, leadership, and strategies is difficult to accomplish.

A second factor is the duration of Ronald Reagan and Jesse Helms in positions of public visibility and political influence. Although considerable grassroots religious-political conservatism lives in the South, much of the force of that movement is attributable to the symbolic leadership of President Reagan. One expects that the notoriety of the NCR's cause will decline when he leaves office (or perhaps early in his second term) and, further, that more centrist Republicans will vie for and take some leadership in the party by the late 1980s. Senator Helms's prominence and his appeal to the Far Right with its wealth and self-assured passion extend his influence well beyond the boundaries of the state he represents. His departure from office will also make a difference. The unique role of each of these men is acknowledged by the repeated statements from the New Christian Right to the effect that the time may be short, because this era presents millennial opportunities that may not last long.

Regionalism in American Religion

EDWIN S. GAUSTAD

For so long in public expression and even longer in private assumption, the prevailing emphasis in American religion as well as in American society was on unity—mainstream, melting pot, consensus religion, the faith of our fathers. Differences were either denied or ignored; variety was either abnormal or dangerous. Unity was all.

Much has changed in this regard within the last generation, as the strength and genius of the nation have been perceived as residing in its diversity. Pluralism has been celebrated rather than denigrated. Minority viewpoints have been sought out, even as minority (and female) representation has been self-consciously encouraged on boards, councils, commissions, and presidential cabinets. This major attitudinal shift has had its clear impact on our understanding of American religion. There, the pattern in the past has been to think almost exclusively in denominational terms, which have more often concealed ethnic and gender diversity than displayed it. Hispanic Catholicism, to take a single example, has been—despite its gigantic size—virtually impotent and invisible until quite recently. "Eastern Orthodoxy" as a phrase suggested to most Americans something foreign and obscure, but the simple label scarcely hinted at the rich ethnic diversity lying underneath. Such bland official names as American Lutheran Church and Lutheran Church in America (and even these are soon to disappear) may represent a real gain in ecumenicity but they lose the nineteenth century's proud assertion of Finnish, Swedish, Danish, Norwegian, and German heritage. In denominational histories through World War II and beyond, the black churches were generally as invisible as their members were in the larger body politic.

All this invisibility in race, in gender, and in ethnic origins has greatly changed in recent times, with the clear result that we look at American religion in the 1980s through quite different eyes. Conferences are held and pastoral letters sent that highlight the place of Hispanic Catholics in America's Roman Catholic church.[1] The "black church" and "slave religion" and "black theology" have all received more scholarly attention in the last 20 years than in the previous 200.[2] And sexist language, along with sexist exclusion of women in roles of leadership in religion, are at least challenged where they have not already disappeared.[3] Never again can one generalize about American religion in ways that suppress or ignore the bountiful and bubbling, and sometimes brawling, ethnic and gender diversity in American religion. The case has been made.

It has been made with such impressiveness, however, that it is in danger of obscuring yet another long-standing source of significant diversity in American religion—its *regional* character. The South is perhaps the one region least in danger of losing its identity as a region, although, as John B. Boles has pointed out, careful and critical scholarship devoted to southern religion is a relatively recent phenomenon.[4] He also notes, however, that this regionalism has quite particular historical roots, such as the Lost Cause cult of the Reconstruction period, and these roots have limited mobility. The "New South," for instance, can no longer be understood in terms applicable to the old Confederacy, for this region extends across west Texas, New Mexico, and Arizona to southern California. There is great difference, to be sure, between Oxford, Mississippi, and Sante Fe, New Mexico; between Charleston, South Carolina, and Los Angeles, California. These glaring contrasts, however, must not blind one to the subtle spread of southern culture throughout the Sunbelt, especially the spread of southern popular religion.

Is regionalism in American religion a phenomenon peculiar to the South? Both historically and contemporaneously, the United States reveals many remarkable examples of regionalism in religion, a regionalism that has implications for community standards in morality, for economic patterns including cultivation of the soil, for public and private education, and even for presidential candidates and the issues that should be mentioned (or omitted) in certain locales.

Colonial Patterns

In considering the colonial period of American history, geography can never be ignored, whether one's attention is on religion or not. No aspect of Virginia's history, for example, can be understood apart from her great rivers. The character of soil and climate shaped New England's pattern of settlement, even as east Jersey was separated from west Jersey as much by the accidents of geography as those of politics. The best known as well as the most enduring religious regionalism of colonial America was that of Puritan New England.[5]

Puritanism made its impact not only upon the land but upon the American mind as well, so that historians speak more confidently of a "New England Way" than they do of any other colonial area. The reasons for this are well known: New Englanders in great numbers were driven by a steady purpose, and they maintained—not by accident but by design—a religious homogeneity that kept church and state connected until well into the nineteenth century. One notes in the accompanying map that New England is as thoroughly blanketed by Congregationalism in 1750 as the rest of the country is almost innocent of Puritanism. The exceptions represent migrations from New England, either overland into New York and New Jersey, or by water to Long Island and even South Carolina. These were mostly exotic plants, however; American Puritanism was rooted in New England and, when the "New England Way" moved across the continent, it drew strength, personnel, and financing largely from Connecticut and Massachusetts.

The Middle Colonies (New York, New Jersey, and Pennsylvania) reveal not one but several religious patterns in the colonial period. No single church dominated; no "Middle Colony Way" has ever been discovered. One can nonetheless find clear patterns by the middle of the eighteenth century, especially within the ranks of the Quakers, the Presbyterians, the Lutherans, and the Dutch and German Reformed. One illustration of this geographical patterning *within* a region (rather than dominating a region) will suffice—the Lutherans.[6] This migration, chiefly from Germany, followed after the earlier migration of English Quakers into west Jersey and Pennsylvania and of Dutch Reformed into New York and east Jersey. Lutherans moved, therefore, back from the coasts, or up the rivers, or even down into the backcountry valleys of Maryland and Virginia. In 1750, however, Lutheranism was almost exclusively a phenomenon of the Middle Colonies—though the reverse, one must remember, was not true. One notes in particular how hostile an environment New England is to Lutheranism. Later immigration would shift the dominance of Lutheranism markedly from its colonial locale.

In the colonial South something like a New England pattern of exclusivity prevailed, though never with the conspicuous success enjoyed in that more northern region. The Church of England, or Anglicanism, enjoyed official patronage and favor in the southern colonies (as, of course, Congregationalism did in New England; Lutheranism did not there or anywhere else). Positively, this meant that government assistance both from England and the colonies themselves aided and abetted the planting and expansion of the Anglican church. Negatively, this meant that governments gave themselves, with varying degrees of vigor and success, to the persecution or prevention of other religious options. The Chesapeake Bay region represents by far the greatest concentration of colonial Anglicanism either in the seventeenth or the eighteenth centuries.[7] As the official church of England, however, this religion could not successfully be excluded anywhere, not even from New England. North Carolina was late to be settled, and even later to be civilized, which is another way of saying that Quakers and Baptists made major inroads there before Anglicanism managed to secure a firm foothold. In the area around Charleston, Anglican parishes were laid out in gratifying numbers and Anglican missionaries arrived in a quantity often more pleasing than the quality; interior South Carolina, however, was hardly penetrated.

Regionalism in American religion is, therefore, not a product of modern times or of sectarian exclusiveness or of secular counterattacks: it is built in from the beginning. Some of that colonial regionalism was fleeting and possibly even irrelevant, but other examples were enduring and of major cultural moment.

Nineteenth–Century Patterns

The opening of the continent in the nineteenth century also promoted religious regionalism. One might expect regionalism to be diluted on the frontier or perhaps even to disappear altogether, thinking that all of the well established groups along the Atlantic seaboard would slowly shift westward, mingling and mixing and losing any geographical identity as they went. For the most part, however, this is not what happened. Some groups were successful on the frontier, others not. Some preferred the urban centers of the East Coast or the well-cleared farmlands of their fathers and mothers. Some waited for education and civilization to go ahead; others saw themselves as the only means by which education and civilization would ever reach the West. And still other prophets and visionaries saw the frontier West as the providential opportunity to start their own church, their new movement, their colony or commune or biblical commonwealth.

For these persons, the East was European and decadent; the West was American and the land of unparalleled religious opportunity. Methodism was a denominational youngster that won its independence about the same time that the nation did. With the bloom of youth still on its cheeks, the new Methodist church set out along post roads and no roads to carry its ministry and message.[8] Across all of New York and Pennsylvania, down the Ohio River to the Mississippi; across the Carolinas and the Appalachian Mountains, down into the deep South; across the Mississippi River into the Ozarks and the piney woods of east Texas, Methodism moved in great force, eventually spreading itself rather evenly all across the Unites States. Even in 1850, it was not exclusively a frontier church as a glance at Maryland, New Jersey, and New England will show. Although certainly a frontier church in part in 1850, it did not rest with that regional identification, with the result that there is no peculiarly Methodist geography today. To highlight, however, the stunning success that Methodism enjoyed on the frontier a century or so ago, its advance can be compared with that of the Episcopal church in the same period.[9] Episcopalians, overly identified with England, had many problems during and after the Revolution; as a result, they were in no position to seize the opportunities presented by the new liberty and the new lands. They were, so to speak, left at the post along the eastern seaboard. While Methodism had entered virtually every county in Georgia, Alabama, and Mississippi, the Episcopal church (which had dominated the South earlier) had made no mark by 1850 in the vast majority of the counties of those three states. In Ohio, Indiana, Illinois, and Missouri, the picture was no better for Methodism's parent church.

For most denominations in nineteenth century America, the move from East to West was a move from the known to the unknown, from the churched to the wholly unchurched. For one denomination, however, this was noticeably not the case. Roman

Catholicism in America was not all Irish, German, and English in 1850: it was heavily Hispanic as well.[10] Santa Fe was settled and missions planted there in 1610 and, although the Spanish were ejected by the Indians later in the seventeenth century, Spain soon returned never to depart culturally or religiously. By 1850 Father Junípero Serra's chain of missions on the Pacific Coast had long been in place. The substitution of a Mexican for a Spanish sovereignty in this region did not erase the Hispanic footsteps, nor did the Anglo conquest that followed result in the replacement of a Hispanic Catholic culture by a Protestant one.

Eastern, "old" Americans often manifested some sense of superiority toward the western, "new" Americans in California after that state was added to the Union in 1850. Such a sense of superiority was totally unjustified, argued English Catholic Herbert Vaughan when he visited California in 1864. To judge a culture, he said, one might note the way in which it treats the native American, the Indian. Here the eastern Americans who came west more for love of gold than love of God did not fare well. Even more conspicuous perhaps, said Father (later Cardinal) Vaughan, was the contrasting attitude toward the land and the names that each group gave to it. The Hispanics named it San Francisco, the Anglos Jackass Gulch; the Hispanics called it Jesus Maria, the Anglos Slap Jack Bar; Hispanics christened it Nuestra Señora de Soledad, the Anglos Skunk Gulch. Herbert Vaughan rested his case.[11] Irrespective of the question of cultural superiority, however, Roman Catholicism was rescued from a regionalism of the northeastern United States largely by a Catholic regionalism of the West, which predated the former by two or more centuries.

To return to the East Coast briefly, there was one other example of regionalism wherein a limiting parochialism (at least geographically) was evident. Unitarianism, which represented a schism within orthodox (Trinitarian) Congregationalism around the end of the eighteenth century, continued to draw its strength from the New England area.[12] Indeed, it was concentrated in, and virtually limited to, New England. Beyond that, a "saturation bombing" occurred in the Boston region giving rise to the old saw that Unitarians believed in the Fatherhood of God, the Brotherhood of Man, and the Neighborhood of Boston. Unitarianism never fully escaped this quite restricted regionalism, but it exercised an influence out of all proportion to its numbers in literature, in social reform, and even in politics. A highly literate fellowship, its power lay not in the control of geography but in the determined exercise of rationality in religion.

Dominant Patterns in the Twentieth Century

Commentators on American society often dwell on the high degree of mobility in the nation today: how few people live in the same house in which they were born, or the same town, or even the same state. Others speak of the homogenization of America by the common influences of television, mass merchandizing, and inside plumbing. From coast to coast, from north to south, Americans are an undifferentiated glob. We all know better, of course, and my only point in overstating the case is to declare that the homogenization has still a very long way to go in religion. At least four "culture religions" can be identified in the 1970s and 80s—the Lutheran in the upper Midwest, the Baptist in the Southeast, the Mormon in the far West, and the Roman Catholic in the Northeast and Southwest.

Lutheranism was a Middle Colony phenomenon in 1750 and almost totally German in ethnicity. Now, a couple of centuries later, both the geography and the ethnicity have shifted. Late nineteenth-century Lutheran immigration was predominantly Scandinavian. The eastern seaboard was full; the upper Midwest was not. This latter region, moreover, represented land and latitude similar to that left behind. The region proved both hospitable and profitable, so much so that the upper Midwest contains (as has often been pointed out) more Swedes than Sweden,

more Norwegians than Norway, more Danes than Denmark, and
so on. But ethnicity often triumphed over theology: that is,
Swedish Lutherans could find more common ground with other
Swedes than with other Lutherans—just as in the eighteenth
century German Lutherans and German Reformed, though from
quite separate theological heritages, sometimes magnified their
common Germanic origin, minimizing their separate theological
ones. Permit me to quote from the grandson of Norwegian immigrants to Minnesota. The communities in that state, he writes,

> were all homogeneous and self-contained. The immigrant in-
> vasion of that part of the country was overwhelmingly Scan-
> dinavian, but the separate components of Scandinavia did not
> become a melting pot in the New World. A township like
> Aastad remained exclusively Norwegian. The Swedes and
> Danes and Finns kept to themselves in communities that had
> names like Swedish Grove and Dane Prairie and Finlandia.
> The different groups could have made themselves understood
> to one another and might have found they had much in com-
> mon. But these exchanges did not occur. . . . Each
> [community] had its own Lutheran churches, newspapers, and
> social fraternities, with little or no cross-pollination. My grand-
> father and my grandmother lived more than sixty and eighty
> years, respectively, but there's no evidence they had more
> than glancing contact with anyone who was not Norwe-
> gian. . . .[14]

Clannishness was as American as apple pie. There was religious
regionalism, but ethnic regionalism even more.

A second example of culture religion today is that of the Baptists. When speaking earlier of frontier regions, the Baptists
could of course have been mentioned along with the Methodists
for they too enjoyed phenomenal success in the sparsely settled
wildernesses. Unlike the Methodists, however, the Baptists
stayed in sufficient force to dominate a huge region south of the
Ohio and Missouri rivers, and on both sides of the Mississippi. In
the state of Mississippi every county but three has more Baptists
than it has members of any other denominational family; in Ala-

bama that same situation obtains in every county but one. Lutheranism's hold on the upper Midwest is not nearly so strong;
that hold is weakened, moreover, by the ethnic division already
noted. The major ethnic division in the Baptist South is, of
course, that between black and white, but the regional dominance would be roughly the same for each group alone. Together,
black Baptists and white Baptists constitute an exceptionally
heavy majority, the precise figures being elusive because of the
paucity of data from the black churches. Of course, Baptists in
this vast region can be and are divided in many ways—
theologically, ecclesiastically, politically, and socially. Fortu-
nately, however, the concern here is only with the concept of
region.

The most convincing example of religious regionalism and geographical "control" in twentieth-century America is that offered
by the Church of Jesus Christ of Latter-day Saints, the Mormons.
In Utah every county is a Mormon county, some to the amazing
extent of 100 percent—no competing religious body at all. The
region has been extended well beyond the Salt Lake Basin into
adjoining states, particularly southern Idaho and western Wyo-
ming. Though Mormonism started in the East (Palmyra, New
York) and paused briefly in the Midwest (Ohio, Illinois, Missouri), the exodus in the late 1840s to Salt Lake City represented
the most striking transplanting in American history of a specific
church from one region of the country to another. The Mormons
encouraged further migrants from the states as well as new converts from abroad and caused the desert to bloom, as the nation's
most successful utopian experiment found in the West a haven
from persecution and harassment as well as a land open to religious conquest. Some observers even speak of "Mormondom," a
term that points to a culture religion of recognizable influence
and proved staying power.

The final dominant pattern in America today is that of Roman
Catholicism, notably in the Northeast (and extending into the old

Northwest) as well as the Southwest, including southern Louisiana (and extending into the Pacific West). The dominance in the Northeast is chiefly a result of European immigration in the nineteenth century, heavily Irish before the Civil War and heavily southern European after that war. French Catholics from Canada have also moved across the border into the United States. Ethnic strains have pulled powerfully at a church seeking to be universal, and they pull still. New York's Archbishop O'Connor and New York's Representative Ferraro no doubt have a real disagreement concerning abortion, but that difference is in no way mitigated by the long standing tensions between Irish Catholic and Italian Catholic. The broad picture of a Roman Catholic region in the Northeast can, upon closer examination, become like the Lutheran region: a mosaic of separate, insular, homogeneous communities or parishes of Catholics who are Irish or German, Italian or Portuguese, French or Polish, Austrian or Puerto Rican, Slavic or Hungarian. In the Southwest, the Hispanic presence accounts for much of the Catholic regionalism there, but certainly not all. The French, of course, dominate the southern half of Louisiana. Indian converts as well as Catholics from the eastern half of the United States also make their presence felt in the whole southwestern corner of the country, and on around to the Pacific Coast. A hierarchical unity gives more force to this regionalism than, say, to the Baptist, but it is a unity mitigated by differing histories, competing ethnic groups, and contending cultural perspectives.

Subtler Patterns in the Twentieth Century

A multi-colored national map may conceal almost as much about American religion as it reveals. Where, for example, are the Presbyterians, the Episcopalians, the Eastern Orthodox, the Jews, the Campbellites, and many others? It is not possible to deal with everyone left after the four macrocultures of Lutherans, Baptists, Mormons, and Catholics have been examined. A few examples of religious geography, however, will indicate that the "big picture" is far from being the total picture. There is a microcosm of religious geography, too, those little worlds sometimes surprising the cross-country highway traveler. While driving across Iowa or Kansas, for example, one may go through a county where the Mennonites are the only significant religious group. Similarly in South Dakota or Montana, one may suddenly be surrounded by nothing but Hutterite farms and Hutterite communities. And if one drives through New England, the Congregational heritage is perfectly plain, so much so that one may too readily conclude that this church still dominates the region. Such is not the case, for Roman Catholicism is the major force there.

Still, Congregationalism (now largely under the name "United Church of Christ") is stronger in New England than anywhere else in the nation.[15] In the mid-twentieth century, one observes Congregationalism moving westward, often in conjunction with Presbyterianism under what was called the Plan of Union. Congregationalism did not, however, move southward in force, with the possible exception of North Carolina. Elsewhere in the South, the Congregational presence reflects vigorous missionary and educational activity among the blacks after the Civil War. Likewise, the New Mexico-Arizona presence largely reflects Congregational missionary work among the Indians in those states—before they became states. The southern California Congregational density represents in part just the huge population of the region but also in part the proclivity of that region to receive its immigrants from all over the nation.

The Dutch Reformed were early to arrive in America, but they arrived from Holland in two waves of immigration widely separated in time. An 1850 map of the Dutch Reformed in America,[16] would show the clear results of that first "invasion" of North America early in the seventeenth century. The New York (which was first New Amsterdam)-New Jersey axis is still clearly defined in 1850, though by this time religious dominance has long since passed to others. By 1950, evidence for that second wave in the nineteenth century is revealed.[17] The Reformed Church in America, as it is now called, is a small church (fewer than ¼ million members), but an influential one partly because its membership is not spread thinly across the nation. Rather, it is concentrated in the upper Midwest where it does actually dominate a few counties, as well as in New York and New Jersey where it no longer controls even its own school, Rutgers University. Unhappily, many of the Dutch Reformed who arrived in the nineteenth century thought that those who had come two centuries earlier were now too much American and too little Dutch This cultural disparity led to schism among the Dutch Calvinists in America; otherwise, their influence would be even stronger. In the study of grouping in American religion, one must pay attention to time as well as to space.

The largest of the Pentecostal churches, Assembly of God, now on its way to 2 million members, is recent in origin (1914) but is developing at a quite rapid pace.[18] It is probably still accurate to think of the Assemblies of God as a southern church, particularly if speaking in terms of the "New South" extending from the Atlantic to the Pacific. The whole nation is exposed to this Pentecostal movement, though, and, by the end of the century, it will probably be more accurate to describe it as a national church.

Among the "subtler patterns," there is a denomination that no longer exists as a separate entity, the Evangelical United Brethren.[19] Often called the "German Methodists," this ethnic group joined with the much larger Methodist church in 1968, the latter appropriating the "United" and making it part of its official title. EUB was clearly a regional church—Pennsylvania, Ohio, and Indiana being the greatest centers of strength. By virtue of such a merger, Methodism greatly strengthened its hand in the Midwest, but hardly altered its status elsewhere in the nation.

Whereas in earlier days, ethnicity was reason enough for a separate organization, that reason became less and less compelling as the twentieth century unrolled. The Roman Catholic regionalism that was discussed before is still evident, though not quite as dramatically so. Yet the Northeast and Southwest still stand out. No state is as sharply bifurcated as Louisiana, with Catholics heavily in the South and Protestants just as heavily in the North, although Texas comes close. The Protestantism of the Midwest and the South is readily apparent; this orientation would be even more "solid" were full data from black churches available. The singular fact about another region, the West, is that church membership as a percentage of total population drops sharply—always excepting the Mormon areas. In California and Oregon less than 25 percent of the population is either Catholic or Protestant, and in both states a few instances are found where the percentage drops below 10 percent. The Gallup polls, which also divide the nation into "regions," tend to confirm the less churched status, and the less church-attending status, of the West.

The South as a Religious Region: the 1980s

As has already been noted, the dominant religion for the South is that of the Baptists. And the dominant specific institution among southern whites is the Southern Baptist Convention, with Alabama and Mississippi enjoying the highest percentage of affiliation (about 30 percent) and Florida the lowest (less than 10 percent). The South's second strongest religious body is Methodism, with the greatest concentration to be found in North Carolina (over 10 percent) and the least in Louisiana (4 percent). Even where Baptists hold the lead on a statewide basis, as in Alabama and Mississippi, Methodists dominate many counties: eight in the former, and nine in the latter. To speak of "dominance" anywhere in the Old Confederate South is to speak almost exclusively of either Baptists or Methodists. The exceptions, to be noted below, are to be found only on the local level and not on the grander or statewide scale.

The Presbyterian Church, U. S., which in 1983 merged with the larger northern body of United Presbyterians, is the third largest denomination in the eleven states of the Confederacy. The Carolinas have the highest percentage of their population in the PCUS (about 3 percent), with Arkansas and Louisiana having the lowest (less than 1 percent). The Presbyterian Church in America, a conservative withdrawal from the PCUS in 1973, has its major base in Alabama and Mississippi; even there, however, the membership expressed as a percentage of the state's total population is only about ½ of 1 percent. The other "mainline" Protestant body that is a visible presence throughout the South is the Episcopal church. This old colonial church fails to dominate any large region, however, serving rather as a significant cultural and religious alternative to the more popular, more broadly based Baptist, Methodist and Presbyterian denominations. The Episcopal church is strongest in Virginia (2.5 percent), weakest in Arkansas (less than 1), but in most states exercises an influence beyond that of its modest numbers.

What of the three other "cultural religions" noted above: Roman Catholics, Lutherans, and Mormons? How do they fare in the South? The Catholics do best, most conspicuously as has been noted in southern Louisiana (over 30 percent of the state's total population is Catholic) and in southern Texas (where Catholic strength brings the whole state's percentage to over 16 percent). But Roman Catholicism is also very strong in south Florida, this concentration being recently enhanced by heavy Cuban immigration. The Gulf Coast counties of Alabama (Mobile and Baldwin) and Mississippi (Hancock, Harrison, and Jackson) also constitute Catholic population centers. Lutheranism has penetrated the South less successfully; with the single exception of Newberry County in South Carolina, it does not dominate any southern county and is least evident in Mississippi. The Mormons control or dominate no southern territory at all, being nowhere more than ½ of 1 percent of the population in any southern state.

If, however, such strong culture religions as Lutheranism and Mormonism have scarcely left their mark, other religious groups not prominent on the national scene find their greatest concentration to be in the South. The Churches of Christ, for example, a conservative separation around the beginning of the twentieth century from the Disciples of Christ movement, are most apparent in the border South, notably in Tennessee (about 5 percent of the population). The Cumberland Presbyterian Church, an early nineteenth century schism, also has its visibility mainly in Tennessee; even there, however, Cumberland Presbyterians are less than 1 percent of the population. The Assemblies of God, as previously observed, are strongest in Arkansas (2.3 percent); other Pentecostal and Holiness groups, on the other hand, flourish in the Carolinas, notably the Church of the Nazarene and the Pentecostal Holiness Church. Fundamentalist Baptist bodies, not affiliated with the Southern Baptist Convention, which also flourish in the South, include the American Baptist Association (over 1 million members) and the Baptist Missionary Association (about one-quarter million members). Arkansas is again the major center of these dissenting Baptists.

Some of the nation's remaining historic religious bodies, whose origins lie outside the South and perhaps even outside the United States, manage to achieve some visibility in specific locales—Judaism in Dade County, Florida; Church of the Brethren in Floyd County, Virginia; the United Church of Christ (Congregational) in much of North Carolina; and the African Methodist Episcopal Zion Church, also strongest in North Carolina but virtually nonexistent in both Arkansas and Texas. The Disciples of Christ have not surrendered all of the South to the Churches of Christ, the former being stronger than the latter in both Virginia and North Carolina. Although the South can in broad terms be described as a region in which Baptists dominate, closer inspection reveals that the patterns of pluralism can be found even here.[21]

Conclusion

What conclusions can be drawn about regionalism in American religion?

1. First, most obviously, religious regionalism has been common, and it is by no means limited to the South.

2. Second, there has been a great deal of tenacity, of endurance, on the part of a religion that has had at any time in its past a strong hold in a specific area: witness the Congregationalists in New England, the Dutch Reformed in New York and New Jersey, and various Germanic faiths in Pennsylvania. A notable exception to this rule, however, is the Anglican or Episcopal church in Virginia. Very strong in all of the Chesapeake region for two hundred years, the modern church is no more powerful there today than it is in most other parts of the country. (One can argue that the historical circumstances here were truly exceptional and that, therefore, the "tenacity rule" still holds.)

3. Third, one can identify at least four powerful "culture religions" in the nation today: that is, religions that so dominate a geographical region that the line between the church and the surrounding culture grows increasingly hard to draw and the force of this unofficial alliance tends to make the religious body ever stronger and more inclusive. The four already identified on a large scale were these: Lutheran, Baptist, Mormon, and Roman Catholic. On a small scale, many more might be added to this list: hamlet by hamlet, valley by valley, county by county.

4. Fouth, one can conclude with a question. I began this paper by suggesting that the days of consensus history and melting-pot sociology appear to be behind us, and that in their respective places we have a celebration of countercultures, diverse perspectives, varied values, and "unmeltable ethnics."[22] We also have

religion by region. Do we pay a price for such regionalism? Is it part of our genius and a source of our strength, or is it only an accident of history and a sketch of fault lines along which great social fissures will eventually appear? Like any proper professor, I raise the questions, leaving you full freedom to provide the answers.

Notes

Notes to INTRODUCTION
by Charles Reagan Wilson

1. Information on most books discussed in this Introduction can be found in the Selected Bibliography at the end of this volume.
2. See John W. Blassingame, *The Slave Community: Plantation Life in the Antebellum South* (New York: Oxford University Press, 1972); Eugene Genovese, *Roll, Jordan, Roll: The World the Slaves Made* (New York: Random House, 1974); George P. Rawick, *From Sundown to Sunup: The Making of the Black Community* (Westport, Conn.: Greenwood Press, 1972); Lawrence W. Levine, *Black Culture and Black Consciousness* (New York: Oxford University Press, 1977); Albert J. Raboteau, *Slave Religion: The "Invisible Institution" in the Antebellum South* (New York: Oxford University Press, 1978).
3. Randall M. Miller and Jon L. Wakelyn, eds., *Catholics in the Old South: Essays on Church and Culture* (Macon, Georgia: Mercer University Press, 1984); Leonard Dinnerstein and Mary Dale Palsson, eds., *Jews in the South* (Baton Rouge: Louisiana State University Press, 1973); Samuel Proctor and Louis Schmier, with Malcolm Stern, eds., *Jews of the South: Selected Essays* (Macon, Georgia: Mercer University Press, 1984).
4. See Robert Moats Miller, "Fourteen Points on the Social Gospel in the South," *Southern Humanities Review* (Summer 1967), 126–140.
5. Tod A. Baker, Robert P. Steed, and Laurence W. Moreland, eds., *Religion and Politics in the South* (New York: Praeger Publishers, 1983).
6. Henry F. May, "The Recovery of American Religious History," *American Historical Review*, 70 (October 1964).
7. Sydney E. Ahlstrom, *A Religious History of the American People* (New Haven: Yale University Press, 1972).
8. James R. Shortridge, "A New Regionalization of American Religion," *Journal for the Scientific Study of Religion*, 16 (June 1977); Edwin S. Gaustad, *Historical Atlas of American Religion* (rev. ed; New York: Harper and Row, 1976).
9. C. Vann Woodward, *The Burden of Southern History* (Baton Rouge: Louisiana State University Press, 1960); Ernest Kurtz, "The Tragedy of Southern Religion," *Georgia Historical Quarterly*, 66 (Summer 1982).

Notes to EVANGELICAL PROTESTANTISM IN THE OLD SOUTH: FROM RELIGIOUS DISSENT TO CULTURAL DOMINANCE
by John B. Boles

1. May, "The Recovery of American Religious History," *American Historical Review* 70 (October 1964), 79–92.
2. See, for example, William Warren Sweet, *The Story of Religion in America* (New York: Harper and Brothers, 1950), 127–54, and esp. 172. The best correc-

tive is Jon Butler, "Enthusiasm Described and Decried: The Great Awakening as Interpretative Fiction," *Journal of American History* 69 (September 1979), 305–325.

3. Ronald W. Long, "Religious Revivalism in the Carolinas and Georgia, 1740–1805" (Ph.D. dissertation, University of Georgia, 1968); David T. Morgan, Jr., "The Great Awakening in the Carolinas and Georgia, 1740–1775" (Ph.D. dissertation, University of North Carolina, 1968); Wesley M. Gewehr, *The Great Awakening in Virginia, 1740–1790* (Durham, N.C.: Duke University Press, 1930).

4. John B. Boles, *The Great Revival in the South, 1787–1805: Origins of the Southern Evangelical Mind* (Lexington, Ky.: University Press of Kentucky, 1972), 1–7.

5. *Ibid.*, 8–9.

6. Clifford Geertz, "Religion as a Cultural System," in Michael P. Banton, ed., *Anthropological Approaches to the Study of Religion* (London: Tavistock Publications, 1966), 1–46.

7. Boles, *Great Revival*, 12–50.

8. *Ibid.*, 37–69; Boles, *Religion in Antebellum Kentucky* (Lexington, Ky.: University Press of Kentucky, 1976), 21–30; Dickson D. Bruce, Jr., *And They All Sang Hallelujah: Plain-Folk Camp-Meeting Religion, 1800–1845* (Knoxville, Tenn.: University of Tennessee Press, 1974), 51–54.

9. See, for example, Anne C. Loveland, *Southern Evangelicals and the Social Order, 1800–1860* (Baton Rouge, La.: Louisiana State University Press, 1980), 65–90.

10. This, of course, is a major theme of Rhys Isaac, *The Transformation of Virginia, 1740–1790* (Chapel Hill, N.C.: University of North Carolina Press, 1982), 161–77.

11. The literature is enormous, but one should sample B. R. White, *The English Separatist Tradition: From the Marian Martyrs to the Pilgrim Fathers* (London: Oxford University Press, 1971), and William G. McLoughlin, *New England Dissent, 1630–1833: The Baptists and the Separation of Church and State* (2 vols., Cambridge, Mass.: Harvard University Press, 1971).

12. Jan Lewis, *The Pursuit of Happiness: Family and Values in Jefferson's Virginia* (Cambridge: Cambridge University Press, 1983), 40–68.

13. James Oakes, *The Ruling Race: A History of American Slaveholders* (New York: Knopf, 1982), 96–122.

14. See Samuel S. Hill, Jr., *Southern Churches in Crisis* (New York: Holt, Rinehart, and Winston, 1966), *passim*, but esp. 73 and 177; Loveland, *Southern Evangelicals*, 91–185, esp. 161–62; Boles, *Great Revival*, 165–203; Edward L. Ayres, *Vengeance and Justice: Crime and Punishment in the 19th-Century American South* (New York: Oxford University Press, 1984), 56–57, 122.

15. Elmer T. Clark *et al.*, eds., *The Journal and Letters of Francis Asbury*, vol. II, *The Journal, 1794 to 1816* (Nashville, 1958), 591 (February 5, 1809).

16. See two articles by Jack P. Maddex, Jr., "From Theocracy to Spirituality: The Southern Presbyterian Reversal on Church and State," *Journal of Presbyterian History* 54 (Winter 1976), 438–57, and "Proslavery Millennialism: Social Eschatology in Antebellum Southern Calvinism," *American Quarterly* 31 (Spring 1979), 46–62. Maddex, however, argues that this conservative social ethic was the norm, not an 1850s aberration as I do. Most of his documentation comes from the 1850s.

17. Winans quoted in Ray Holder, *William Winans: Methodist Leader in An-*

tebellum Mississippi (Jackson, Miss.: University Press of Mississippi, 1977), 148. Palmer's views are expressed in "Thanksgiving Sermon, Delivered . . . in New Orleans, on Thursday, November 29, 1860 . . . ," reprinted in B. M. Palmer and W. T. Leacock, eds., *The Rights of the South Defended in the Pulpits* (Mobile: J. Y. Thompson, 1860), 1–16, and *A Vindication of Secession and the South* . . . (Columbia, S.C.: Southern Guardian Steam-Power Press, 1861).

18. My discussion of slavery is adapted from my *Black Southerners, 1619–1869* (Lexington, Ky.: University Press of Kentucky, 1983), 153–68; see also David T. Bailey, "Slavery and the Churches: The Old Southwest" (Ph.D. dissertation, University of California at Berkeley, 1979), 143–63; Kenneth K. Bailey, "Protestantism and Afro-Americans in the Old South: Another Look," *Journal of Southern History* 41 (November 1975), 451–72; Larry James, "Slaves and Baptist Churches in Antebellum Mississippi," paper read at the Southern Historical Association, November 13, 1981; and "A Mingled Yarn: Biracial Churches in Amite County, Mississippi, 1800–1870," unpublished paper by Randy Sparks, Rice University, October 1984. The older view of the slaves' religion as simply an opiate to make them forget their pains on earth, or a heavy-handed attempt by whites to control their hapless bondsmen, is largely recognized today as a caricature of black history. Recent research indicates that the normative worship experience of slaves was in a biracial church, where—despite clear inequalities and white prejudice—blacks heard the full gospel preached and achieved a significant degree of spiritual freedom. Only in those special portions of the sermons specifically directed toward them—much as so-called children's sermons in many churches today—did slaves hear emphasized the truncated gospel of "slaves obey your master." The similarity in theology and ecclesiology of the post-Civil War independent black denominations to the antebellum "white" denominations from which they withdrew suggests the authenticity of the biracial worship experiences.

19. Catherine Clinton discusses southern women and religion briefly in *The Plantation Mistress: Woman's World in the Old South* (New York: Pantheon, 1982), 95–96, 152, 157–58, and esp. 160–63. Suzanne Lebsock in *The Free Women of Petersburg: Status and Culture in a Southern Town, 1784–1860* (New York: Norton, 1984), 214–28, more nearly represents my view. See also Anne Firor Scott, *The Southern Lady: From Pedestal to Politics, 1830–1930* (Chicago: University of Chicago Press, 1970), 10–13, 42–43.

20. See the unpublished paper by Elizabeth H. Turner, "Equality in Christ: A Social History of the First Baptist Church of Galveston, 1840–1861," Rice University, September 1984.

21. Woodward, "Introduction" to the paperback edition of *Life and Labor in the Old South* by Ulrich Bonnell Phillips (Boston: Little, Brown, 1963), v–vi.

Notes to THE BLACK HERITAGE IN RELIGION IN THE SOUTH
by C. Eric Lincoln

*Adapted in part from C. Eric Lincoln, *Race, Religion, and the Continuing American Dilemma* (New York: Hill and Wang, 1984).

1. See Clyde Ahmad Winters, "Afro-American Muslims from Slavery to Freedom," *Islamic Studies*, 17 (No. 4, 1978), 187–190.

2. Allan D. Austin, *African Muslims in Antebellum America* (New York: Garland Publishing, Inc., 1984).
3. *The Atlanta University Publications* (New York: Arno Press and the New York Times, 1968), 11.
4. *Ibid.*, 22.
5. See Lorenzo J. Greene, *The Negro In Colonial New England* (New York: Atheneum, 1968), 186.
6. Winthrop Jordon, *White Over Black* (Chapel Hill: University of North Carolina Press, 1968), 186.
7. Greene, *Negro in Colonial New England*, 276.
8. Hortense Powdermaker, *After Freedom* (New York: Atheneum, 1968), 227.
9. *The Atlanta University Publications*, 27.
10. *Ibid.*, 29–30.
11. *The Atlanta University Publications*, 36.
12. C.f., Carter G. Woodson and Charles H. Wesley, *The Negro in Our History* (Washington, D.C., Associated Publishers), 156.
13. For details on John Chavis and Joseph Evans, see C. Eric Lincoln, "Black Religion In North Carolina from Colonial Times to 1900," in Jeffrey T. Crow and Robert E. Winters, eds., *The Black Presence in North Carolina* (Raleigh: The North Carolina Museum of History, 1978), 9–24.

Notes to RELIGIOUS PLURALISM: CATHOLICS, JEWS, AND
SECTARIANS
by David Edwin Harrell, Jr.

1. Samuel S. Hill, ed., *Religion in the Southern States* (Macon, Ga.: Mercer University Press, 1983), 1–2.
2. John B. Boles, "Religion in the South: Recent Historiography" (unpublished paper delivered at the meeting of the Southern Historical Association, Nov. 6, 1982), 34. See Edwin S. Gaustad, *Historical Atlas of Religion in America* (Rev. ed.; New York: Harper and Row, 1976), 48–51, 122–128.
3. (Rev. ed.; Ft. Worth: Noble Patterson, Publisher-Distributor, 1975), xii.
4. Hill, ed., *Religion in the Southern States*, 101.
5. Jon L. Wakelyn and Randall M. Miller, eds., *Catholics in the Old South* (Mercer, Ga.: Mercer University Press [1983]), 7.
6. See Eli N. Evans, *The Provincials* (New York: Antheneum, 1974), 252; Fedora Small Frank, *Beginnings on Market Street, Nashville and Her Jewry, 1861–1901* ([Nashville]: Frank, 1976), 111. See also Charles Riznikoff and Uriah Z. Engelman, *The Jews of Charleston* (Philadelphia: Jewish Publication Society of America, 1950); Mark H. Elovitz, *A Century of Jewish Life in Dixie: The Birmingham Experience* (University, Ala.: University of Alabama Press, [1974]); Bertram Wallace Korn, *The Early Jews of New Orleans* (Waltham, Mass.: American Jewish Historical Society, 1969); Myron Berman, *Richmond's Jewry, 1769–1976* (Charlottesville, Va.: University Press of Virginia [1979]).
7. Leonard Dinnerstein and Mary Dale Palsson, eds., *Jews in the South* (Baton Rouge: Louisiana State University Press, 1973), 3.
8. Isaac's descriptions of the Baptists could be taken as accounts of twentieth-century southern sects: "The Baptists' appearance was austere, to be sure, but we

shall not understand the deep appeal of the evangelical movement, or the nature and full extent of its pointed negation of the style and vision of the gentry-oriented social world, unless we look into the rich offerings beneath this somber exterior. Converts were proffered some escape from the harsh realities of disease, debt, overindulgence and deprivation, violence and fear of sudden death, that were the common lot of small farmers. They could seek refuge in a close, support-ive, and orderly community. . . ." Rhys Isaac, *The Transformation of Virginia* (Chapel Hill, N.C.: The University of North Carolina Press [1982]), 164; see 163–172.

9. C. Vann Woodward, *Origins of the New South, 1877–1913* ([Baton Rouge]: Louisiana State University Press, 1951). For a summary of that literature, see Lacy K. Ford, "Rednecks and Merchants: Economic Development and Social Tensions in the South Carolina Upcountry, 1865–1900," *Journal of American History*, 71 (September 1984), 294–318.

10. "Rednecks and Merchants," 298.

11. Wukulja und Miller eds., *Catholics in the Old South*, 35.

12. Lorenzo Dow, *The Dealings of God, Man and the Devil As Exemplified in the Life, Experience and Travels of Lorenzo Dow.* . . (2 vols,; New York: Cornish, Lamport & Co., 1851), II, 165–166.

13. *Southern Evangelicals and the Social Order, 1800–1860* (Baton Rouge and London: Louisiana State University Press [1980]), 33.

14. *Minutes of the Annual Conference of the Methodist Episcopal Church, South, for the Year 1863* (Nashville: Southern Methodist Publishing House, 1870), 467.

15. *A History of the Baptist Churches in the United States* (6th ed., rev. and enlarged; Philadelphia: American Baptist Publication Society, 1915), 320.

16. Abel Stevens, *A Compendious History of American Methodism* (New York: Hunt & Eaton [1867]), 552.

17. "The Antimission Movement in the Jacksonian South: A Study in Regional Folk Culture," *Journal of Southern History*, 36 (November 1970), 502; see 501–529.

18. Robert A. Baker, *The Southern Baptist Convention and Its People, 1607–1972* (Nashville: Broadman Press [1974]), 152.

19. Robert G. Torbet, *A History of the Baptists* (rev. ed.; Valley Forge: The Judson Press, 1969), 273. See Newman, *Baptist Churches*, 437, 440.

20. Wyatt-Brown, "The Antimission Movement," 516.

21. David Benedict, *A General History of the Baptist Denomination.* . . . (New York: Lewis Colby and Company, 1849), 935.

22. See Baker, *Southern Baptist Convention*, 208–219; William Wright Barnes, *The Southern Baptist Convention, 1845–1953* (Nashville: Broadman Press [1954]), 103–117; James E. Tull, "A Study of Southern Baptist Landmarkism in the Light of Historical Baptist Ecclesiology" (Ph.D. dissertation, Columbia Uni-versity, 1960); Hugh Wamble, "Landmarkism: Doctrinaire Ecclesiology Among Baptists," *Church History*, 33 (December 1964), 429–444.

23. Wamble, "Landmarkism," 348.

24. Charles Reagan Wilson, *Baptized in Blood* (Athens: The University of Geor-gia Press, 1980).

25. "Why the South is Anti-Evolution," *The World's Work*, 50 (September 1925), 552.

26. *The Making of a Southerner* (New York: Alfred A. Knopf, 1947), 162–163.

27. Quoted in Baker, *Southern Baptist Convention*, 277.
28. "Why the South is Anti-Evolution," 549. Also see Gerald W. Johnson, "The Battling South," *Scribner's Magazine*, 77 (March 1925), 307.
29. W. P. Trent, "Tendencies of Higher Life in the South," *Atlantic Monthly*, 79 (June 1897), 777–778.
30. Ralph E. Morrow, "Introduction," in Emory Stevens Bucke, ed., *The History of American Methodism* (3 vols.; New York and Nashville: Abingdon Press [1964]), II, 592–593.
31. Jeremiah Bell Jeter, *The Recollections of a Long Life* (Richmond: The Religious Herald Co., 1891), 310–319.
32. U.S. Bureau of the Census, *Religious Bodies: 1916* . . . (2 vols.; Washington, D.C.: Government Printing Office, 1919), I, 121.
33. Newman, *Baptist Churches in the United States*, 383.
34. W. Morgan Patterson, "The Influence of Landmarkism Among Baptists," *Baptist History and Heritage*, 11 (January 1976), 44–45.
35. Baker, *Southern Baptist Convention*, 278.
36. See Wamble, "Landmarkism," 444; William E. Ellis, "The Fundamentalist-Modernist Schism Over Evolution in the 1920's," *Register* of the Kentucky Historical Society, 74 (April 1976), 114–116.
37. Patterson, "Influence of Landmarkism," 54.
38. Wamble, "Landmarkism," 444.
39. See Baker, *Southern Baptist Convention*, 284.
40. U.S. Bureau of the Census, *Religious Bodies: 1926* . . . (Washington, D.C.: Government Printing Office, 1930), II, 224–227, 104.
41. See Timothy L. Smith, *Revivalism and Social Reform in Mid-Nineteenth Century America* (New York and Nashville: Abingdon Press [1957]), 135–147.
42. Duncan Aikman, "The Holy Rollers," *American Mercury*, 15 (no. 58, 1928), 183. For general information on the Holiness movement see Timothy L. Smith, *Called Unto Holiness: The Story of the Nazarenes* (Kansas City: Nazarene Publishing House, 1962); Robert Mapes Anderson, *Vision of the Disinherited: The Making of American Pentecostalism* (New York and Oxford: Oxford University Press, 1979); and Timothy L. Smith, "The Holiness Crusade," in Bucke, ed., *History of American Methodism*, II, 608–627.
43. Contrary to the general denominational pattern, most of the Nazarene churches in the South were rural. *Religious Bodies: 1926*, II, 383–385. See Charles Edwin Jones, "Disinherited or Rural? A Historical Case Study in Urban Holiness Religion," *Missouri Historical Review*, 76 (April 1972), 395–412; Vinson Synan, *The Holiness-Pentecostal Movement in the United States* (Grand Rapids, Michigan: William B. Eerdmans Publishing Company [1971]), 75.
44. Smith, "The Holiness Crusade," 615.
45. *Holiness-Pentecostal Movement*, 39.
46. Quoted in Frederick A. Bode, *Protestantism and the New South* (Charlottesville: University Press of Virginia [1975]), 150.
47. See Anderson, *Vision*, 35.
48. *Religious Bodies: 1916*, II, 633–637, 989.
49. Quoted in Ben Barrus, Milton L. Baughn and Thomas H. Campbell, *A People Called Cumberland Presbyterians* (Memphis: Frontier Press [1972]), 341.
50. See *ibid.*, 375, 376; *Religious Bodies: 1916*, I, 348.
51. *Religious Bodies: 1916*, II, 572; Barrus, *et al.*, *A People Called Cumberland Presbyterians*, 332.

52. See David Edwin Harrell, Jr., "The Sectional Origins of the Churches of Christ," *Journal of Southern History*, 30 (August 1964), 261–277.

53. *Religious Bodies: 1916*, I, 365, 366, 386, 428, 438, 443, 444.

54. *Ibid.*, 121.

55. *Ibid.*, 209, 249.

56. Daniel Sommer, "The Signs of the Times," *Octographic Review*, 40 (October 5, 1897), 1. See David Edwin Harrell, Jr., *The Social Sources of Division in the Disciples of Christ, 1865–1900* (Atlanta and Athens: Publishing Systems, Inc. [1973]), 323–350.

57. "The Church as God Ordained It," *Gospel Advocate*, 38 (July 9, 1896), 436.

58. "Why the South is Anti-Evolution," 551.

59. *A Mencken Chrestomathy* (New York: Alfred A. Knopf, 1974), 398.

60. See Anderson, *Vision*, p. 175.

61. The southern Pentecostal churches were unquestionably predominately Methodist in origin and doctrine. On the other hand, the Assemblies of God, which was less a southern church, revealed clear Baptist influence on its early beliefs and practices. For discussions of this interesting point, see Anderson, *Vision*, 153–175; Edith Lydia Waldvogel, "'The 'Overcoming Life': A Study in the Reformed Evangelical Origins of Pentecostalism" (Ph.D. dissertation, Harvard University, 1977); Synan, *Holiness-Pentecostal Movement*, 147–153.

62. See Synan, *Holiness-Pentecostal Movement*, 73, 131. Synan says that "many southern Baptist members also became converts to the pentecostal religion."

63. *Religious Bodies: 1916*, II, 40–42.

64. *Ibid.*, 210–213.

65. *Discipline of the Pentecostal Holiness Church, 1937* (Franklin Springs, Georgia: Publishing House of the Pentecostal Holiness Church [1937]), 12–43.

66. Aikman, "The Holy Rollers," 191.

67. See Jones, "Disinherited or Rural," 400.

68. *Discipline of the Pentecostal Holiness Church, 1937*, 42.

69. *Ibid.*

70. Raymond Othel Corvin, "Religious and Educational Backgrounds in the Founding of Oral Roberts University" (Ph.D. dissertation, University of Oklahoma, 1967), 275.

71. Aikman, "The Holy Rollers," 191.

72. See Synan, *Holiness-Pentecostal Movement*, 187.

73. Bode, *Protestantism and the New South*, 7. Also see Frederick Bode, "Religion and Class Hegemony: A Populist Critique in North Carolina," *Journal of Southern History*, 38 (August 1971), 417–438.

74. Quoted in Francis Butler Simkins, *The Everlasting South* ([Baton Rouge]: Louisiana State University Press [1963]), 82.

75. Liston Pope, *Millhands and Preachers* (New Haven: Yale University Press, 1942), 138.

76. Historical Records Survey, Arkansas, Records Inventory Files, 1936–1942, Box 415, Special Collections, University of Arkansas.

77. *Ibid.*, Box 413.

78. *Ibid.*, Box 446.

79. Wakelyn and Miller, eds., *Catholics in the Old South*, 246.

Notes to "FEEDING THE HUNGRY AND MINISTERING TO THE BROKEN
HEARTED: THE PRESBYTERIAN CHURCH IN THE UNITED STATES
AND THE SOÇIAL GOSPEL, 1900–1920"
by J. Wayne Flynt

I wish to acknowledge with gratitude the support given this project by an
Auburn University research grant and the invaluable assistance of Dr.
Jerrold Brooks and his staff at the Historical Foundation of the Presbyterian and Re-
formed Churches at Montreat, North Carolina.
    1. Walter L. Lingle, *The Bible and Social Problems* (New York: Fleming H.
Revell Co., 1929), 7.
    2. *Minutes of the General Assembly of the Presbyterian Church in the United
States, 1911* (Richmond, Virginia: Presbyterian Committee of Publication, 1911),
27. Hereafter cited as *Minutes, PCUS. Ibid., 1910*, 60; A. L. Phillips to W. L.
Lingle, May 24, 1911, Walter L. Lingle Papers, Historical Foundation of the
Presbyterian and Reformed Churches, Montreat, North Carolina. Hereafter
cited as Lingle Papers.
    3. For a splendid article on the nuances of the Social Gospel, see Winthrop S.
Hudson, "Walter Rauschenbusch and the New Evangelism," *Religion in Life*, 30
(Summer 1961), 412–430.
    4. *Ibid.;* for example, see Shailer Mathews, *The Social Teaching of Jesus: An
Essay in Christian Sociology* (New York: Hodder and Stoughton, 1897).
    5. See Walter Rauschenbusch, *Christianity and The Social Crisis* (New York:
The Macmillan Company, 1907).
    6. In an excellent recent book entitled *The Social Gospel in the South: The
Woman's Home Mission Movement in the Methodist Episcopal Church South,
1886–1939* (Baton Rouge: Louisiana State University Press, 1982), John P.
McDowell briefly surveys the literature. Ronald C. White, Jr., and C. Howard
Hopkins recognize the presence of such a southern dimension in their book, *The
Social Gospel: Religion and Reform in Changing America* (Philadelphia: Temple
University Press, 1976), which contains a useful chapter, "Voices from the New
South." Dewey W. Grantham's excellent study, *Southern Progressivism: The
Reconciliation of Progress and Tradition* (Knoxville: The University of Tennessee
Press, 1983), discusses the Social Gospel in a chapter entitled "Social Justice."
There and in his final chapter, "The Reconciliation of Progress and Tradition," he
properly limits the extent of commitment to change while arguing that progres-
sives were reformers seeking social justice. Southern churchmen played a major
role in his chronicle of reform.
    7. John B. Boles and Samuel S. Hill presently argue that though the Social
Gospel existed in the South it was of little consequence and existed largely "on
the very fringes of southern Protestantism" (to use Boles's term), or that the Social
Gospel "has been present in only minor and occasional forms, and never dominant" (to use Hill's term). Ronald C. White, Jr., although willing to concede the
existence of the Social Gospel in the South in his 1976 work, was not so sure in
1984. Reviewing McDowell's book, he suggests that McDowell perhaps confused
social concern with the Social Gospel and that no linkage is made between ideas
and actions. See John B. Boles, "Religion in the South: Recent Historiography,"
paper presented at the Southern Historical Association, November 6, 1982;
Samuel S. Hill's review of McDowell's book, *The Journal of Southern History*, 50
(February 1984), 139–140; and Ronald C. White's review of McDowell's book in
Church History, 53 (June 1984), 268.

8. Ruth Hutchinson Crocker, "Sympathy and Science: The Settlement Movement in Gary and Indianapolis to 1930" (Ph.D. dissertation, Purdue University, 1982), especially 482–483. The extent of religious settlement house work in Gary and Indianapolis appears to be roughly comparable to that in Birmingham and Atlanta, although in 1911 only 45 of the nation's 413 settlement houses were in the South. But this percentage does not deviate substantially from the South's proportion of major cities.

9. See Hugh C. Bailey, *Liberalism in the New South: Southern Social Reformers and the Progressive Movement* (Coral Gables: University of Miami Press, 1969); Morton Sosna, *In Search of the Silent South: Southern Liberals and the Race Issue* (New York: Columbia University Press, 1977); Anthony P. Dunbar, *Against The Grain: Southern Radicals and Prophets, 1929–1959* (Charlottesville, Virginia: University of Virginia Press, 1981).

10. See T. Scott Miyakawa, *Protestants and Pioneers: Individualism and Conformity on the American Frontier* (Chicago: The University of Chicago Press, 1964), 4.

11. See Ernest T. Thompson, *Presbyterians in the South, Vol. II, 1861–1890* (Richmond: John Knox Press, 1965), 413; *ibid., Vol. III, 1890–1972* (Richmond: John Knox Press, 1973), especially 265–269.

12. S. R. Church to W. L. Lingle, March 13, 1914; S. W. Carson to W. L. Lingle, June 5, 1913; Lingle Papers.

13. R. E. Magill to W. L. Lingle, April 14, 1911, Lingle Papers; *Minutes of the PCUS, 1912*, 42; *ibid., 1920*, 63–64.

14. E. T. Thompson discusses the doctrine of the Spirituality of the Church thoroughly in his three volumes on the PCUS.

15. *Minutes of the PCUS, 1907*, 57; *ibid., 1910*, 44–45; *ibid., 1915*, 29.

16. W. L. Lingle to Dr. John T. Thomas, December 30, 1916, Lingle Papers.

17. D. P. McGeachy to W. L. Lingle, undated but probably in 1915 or 1916, Lingle Papers.

18. Quoted in Bailey, *Liberalism in the New South*, 179–180.

19. *Ibid.*, scattered throughout, and Grantham, *Southern Progressivism*, 191–199.

20. *Minutes of the PCUS, 1908*, 19.

21. James R. Howerton, *The Church and Social Reforms* (New York: Fleming H. Revell, 1913), quotation on 83.

22. *Ibid.*, see especially his final chapter.

23. Thompson, *Presbyterians in the South, Vol. III*, 101–105; David E. Whisnant, *All That Is Native and Fine* (Chapel Hill: The University of North Carolina Press, 1983), 37–39; *Minutes of the PCUS, 1914*, 43; *ibid., 1916*, 12.

24. Thompson, *Presbyterians in the South, Vol. III*, 105; *Minutes of the PCUS, 1914*, 104.

25. For such views, see Elizabeth R. Hooker, *Religion in the Highlands: Native Churches and Missionary Enterprises in the Southern Appalachian Area* (New York: The Home Missions Council, 1933).

26. *Minutes of the PCUS, 1916*, 31; *ibid., 1914*, 43; *ibid., 1917*, 105–106; "Minutes of the Home Mission Board," Research Center of the Historical Foundation, PCUS, Montreat, North Carolina, February 15, 1910; *ibid.*, 1910–1913. Hereafter cited as "Minutes of the Home Mission Board."

27. See John C. Campbell, *The Future of the Churches and Independent Schools in our Southern Highlands* (New York: Russell Sage Foundation, 1917); Mrs. Olive D. Campbell, *Southern Highland Schools Maintained by Denomina-*

tional and Independent Agencies (New York: Russell Sage Foundation, 1921); O. D. Campbell, *The Life and Work of John Charles Campbell* (Madison: University of Wisconsin Press, 1968).

28. "Minutes of the Home Mission Board, 1911," 60–61, 76–77, 106, 127, 153, 180, 185; *Minutes of the PCUS, 1912*, 44; *ibid., 1913*, 58.

29. W. E. Hudson to W. L. Lingle, January 14, 1915, Lingle Papers; G. E. Drushal to Edward O. Guerrant, August 17, 1915, Edward O. Guerrant Papers, Research Center of the Historical Foundation, PCUS, Montreat, North Carolina.

30. "Appalachia" file, Henry H. Sweets Papers, Historical Foundation of the Presbyterian and Reformed Churches, Montreat, North Carolina; William E. Hudson, *'The Least of These': The Beneficenses of the Synod of Virginia* (Richmond: Presbyterian Committee of Publications, 1926), 113–114; William E. Hudson to W. L. Lingle, February 28, 1914; E. E. Lane to W. L. Lingle, January 30, 1913; R. E. Magill to W. L. Lingle, January 12, 1909; all in Lingle Papers; Rev. Edward Marshall Craig, *Highways and Byways of Appalachia: A Study of the Work of the Synod of Appalachia of the Presbyterian Church in the United States* (Kingsport, Tennessee: n.p., 1927), 67.

31. Mary N. Sloop to W. L. Lingle, ? 23, 1918, Lingle Papers; *Minutes of the PCUS, 1917*, 107; Ora C. Huston to W. L. Lingle, July 21, 1919, and H. A. Love to W. L. Lingle, February 11, 1918; Lingle Papers.

32. Edward O. Guerrant, *The Galax Gatherers: The Gospel Among the Highlanders* (Richmond: Onward Press, 1910), especially 59.

33. *Ibid.*, 73–76, 182–183.

34. Ora C. Huston to W. L. Lingle, September 10, 1919, Lingle Papers.

35. William E. Hudson, *'The Least of These,'* 60–65; "Students Who have Attended the Assembly's Training School," 1916–17, ms. in Lingle Papers; Helen Mathews to W. L. Lingle, May 11 and 14, 1920, Lingle Papers.

36. Mary M. Sloop to W. L. Lingle, ? 23, 1918, and February 12, 1918; Lingle Papers.

37. Rev. R. P. Smith, *Experiences in Mountain Mission Work* (Richmond: Presbyterian Committee on Publications, 1931), 46, 61.

38. For examples of the rural expression of Progressivism and the Social Gospel, see William L. Bowers, *The Country Life Movement in America, 1900–1920* (Port Washington, New York: Kennikat Press, 1974).

39. James Williams Marshall, *The Presbyterian Church in Alabama*, edited by Robert Strong (Montgomery: The Presbyterian Historical Society of Alabama, 1977), 288; Stanford Binkley to W. L. Lingle, November 28, 1913; W. L. Downing to W. L. Lingle, February 18, 1918; Lingle Papers.

40. R. E. Magill to W. L. Lingle, January 6, 1908, Lingle Papers; "Minutes of Home Mission Board," November, 1910, 41.

41. Willis Thompson to W. L. Lingle, October 13, 1914; A. L. Phillips to W. L. Lingle, February 20, 1915; Lingle Papers.

42. Willis Thompson to W. L. Lingle, October 13, 1914, Lingle Papers.

43. For Lingle's reading of Wilson, see W. L. Lingle to Dr. A. P. Bourland, March 20, 1915, Lingle Papers. For a sample of Wilson's ideas on the rural church, see Warren H. Wilson, *The Church of the Open Country* (New York: Missionary Education Movement of the United States and Canada, 1911), and Wilson, *The Church at the Center* (New York: Missionary Education Movement of the United States and Canada, 1914).

44. Warren H. Wilson to Walter L. Lingle, October 20, 1914; A. P. Bourland to W. L. Lingle, April 2, 1915; copy of "The Southern Conference for Education and

Industry, Chattanooga, April 27th–30th, 1915"; all in Lingle Papers.
45. Copy of brochure, "Montreat N. C. Program, 1916," in Lingle Papers; Rev.
W. H. Mills, "The Church's Duty To the Country Church," *Union Seminary Review* (W. L. Lingle, editor), 31 (October 1919–July 1920), 39–45.
46. F. Wade Vaughan to W. L. Lingle, March 31, 1908; Gracy W. Hampton to
W. L. Lingle, October 29, 1911; Lingle Papers.
47. *Minutes of the PCUS, 1911*, 33–34.
48. "Minutes of the Home Mission Board," May 12, 1908, 122; *ibid.*, December
15, 1908, 136–137; *ibid.*, March 9, 1909, 143; *ibid.*, May 11, 1909, 149; *ibid.*,
October 12, 1909, 160–161; *ibid.*, October 11, 1910, 38.
49. For a thorough discussion of racial views within the PCUS, see Joel Alvis,
"The Bounds of Their Habitations: The Southern Presbyterian Church, Racial
Ideology and Civil Rights, 1945–1972" (Ph.D. dissertation, Auburn University,
forthcoming).
50. Rev. II. H. Proctor to Walter Lingle, October 4, 1910; Marjorie Gray to
Walter Lingle, undated but probably 1910; Lingle Papers; and Alvis, "The
Bounds of Their Habitations."
51. Nolan R. Best to W. L. Lingle, July 14, 1900, Lingle Papers; Thompson,
Presbyterians in the South, Vol. III: 1890–1972, 265.
52. Quoted in Lingle, *The Bible and Social Problems*, 12–13.
53. *Ibid.*, 29–32; W. L. Lingle to George H. Doran Co., November 28, 1913;
William T. Hanzsche to W. L. Lingle, February 27, 1918, and Lingle to
Hanzsche, March 2, 1918; Lingle Papers.
54. J. L. Hughes to W. L. Lingle, March 20, 1917; Lingle to Hughes, April 25,
1917; for a similar letter referring a reader to Social Gospel materials, see Lingle
to Stanley White, April 20, 1918; Lingle Papers.
55. List of "Books on Home Missions," in Lingle Papers; W. L. Lingle to J. S.
Lyons, June 23, 1913; W. L. Lingle to R. M. Russell, June 25, 1913; Lingle
Papers.
56. "The Bible and Money," "Wealth and Social Problems," "Poverty and Social
Problems," sermon manuscripts in Lingle Papers.
57. "The Family and Social Problems," "Christianity and the Race Problem,"
sermon and discussion outline in Lingle Papers.
58. J. J. Hill to W. L. Lingle, September 15, 1916; E. D. Brown to W. L.
Lingle, April 20, 1916; Lingle Papers.
59. A. W. McAlister to W. L. Lingle, December 14 and 20, 1915; Margaret E.
Burton to W. L. Lingle, March 11 and May 21, 1918, Lingle to Burton, March 19,
1918; W. L. Lingle to R. A. Swink, May 17, 1920; Lingle Papers.
60. John T. Farris to W. L. Lingle, June 29, 1916, Lingle Papers.
61. Lingle, *The Bible and Social Problems*, 176–177, 191.
62. Thompson, *Presbyterians in the South, Vol. III: 1890–1972*, 265–266.
63. *Ibid.*, 268–269.
64. "Minutes of the Home Mission Board," April 5, 1910, April 4, 1911; *Minutes
of the PCUS, 1911*, 84–85; *ibid., 1914*, 107–108; *Presbyterian Standard*, February
13, 1918.
65. D. W. Brannen to W. L. Lingle, January 3, 1910, Lingle Papers.
66. *Minutes of the PCUS, 1912*, 62–63; *ibid.*, 1915, 80d.
67. *Ibid.*, 1911, 30; *ibid.*, 1912, 64; *ibid.*, 1913, 70n–70p; *ibid.*, 1914, 26–28.
68. Programs for Montreat Conferences for 1916 and 1917, copies in Lingle
Papers.
69. Head to Lingle, January 16, 1913; W. Bruce Buford to W. L. Lingle, April

28, 1914; A. D. Wauchope to W. L. Lingle, March 4, 1915; James H. Henderlite to W. L. Lingle, February 23, 1915 and January 29, 1917; W. L. Lingle to Rev. A. B. Bass, January 29, 1918; Lingle Papers.
70. *Presbyterian Standard,* August 14, 1912.
71. *Ibid.,* August 14, 1912, January 30, February 27, April 17, October 9, 1918, March 19, 1919.
72. W. H. Lingle to W. L. Lingle, September 8 and June 13, 1917; Margaret Lingle to W. L. Lingle, April 29, 1917; Lingle Papers.
73. Lingle, *The Bible and Social Problems,* 162.
74. *Minutes of the PCUS, 1919,* 87–88.
75. See Lois A. Boyd and R. Douglas Brackenridge, "The Evolving Role of the Southern Presbyterian Woman: Blessed Inconsistencies," *Presbyterian Women in America: Two Centuries of a Quest for Status* (Westport, Connecticut: Greenwood Press, 1983), 207–208; *Minutes of the PCUS, 1897,* 16.
76. Quoted in Thompson, *Presbyterians in the South, Vol. III: 1890–1972,* 387–388.
77. *Minutes of the PCUS, 1911,* 67.
78. L. Sorrows to W. L. Lingle, undated but in 1915, Lingle Papers.
79. Thompson, *Presbyterians in the South, Vol. III: 1890–1972,* 388–389; *Presbyterian Standard,* May 15, 1912.
80. *Presbyterian Standard,* May 8 and May 15, 1912; "Minutes of Home Mission Board," December 12, 1911, 115, and January 9, 1912, 119; *Minutes of the PCUS, 1912,* 60.
81. See Hallie Paxson Winsborough, *The Woman's Auxiliary Presbyterian Church U.S.* (Richmond: Presbyterian Committee of Publication, 1927); *Minutes of the PCUS, 1914,* 38, 62; *ibid., 1913,* 58, 70d; (Mrs.) W. C. Winsborough to W. L. Lingle, March 23, 1918, Lingle Papers.
82. *Minutes of the PCUS, 1913,* 33; *Ibid., 1919,* 31–32; *ibid., 1920,* 20; S. L. Morris to W. L. Lingle, April 30, 1918; Neal L. Anderson to W. L. Lingle, November 19, 1919; Lingle Papers.
83. W. C. S. to Rev. T. C. Johnson, May 5, 1914, Lingle Papers; *Minutes of the PCUS, 1916,* 48–49, 76–77, 80a–80b; *ibid., 1917,* 68–69.
84. *Presbyterian Standard,* May 29, September 18, and October 16, 1918, February 4 and March 3, 1920.
85. Thomas W. Lingle to W. L. Lingle, February 19, 1915; Clara L. Lingle to W. L. Lingle, October 3, 1917; Montreat Program Schedule, 1918; all in Lingle Papers.
86. W. L. Lingle to T. W. Lingle, March 11, 1916; T. W. Lingle to W. L. Lingle, March 14, 1916; Lingle Papers.
87. Eugene Alexander to W. L. Lingle, May 2, 1918; W. L. Lingle to Charles R. Hemphill, November 24, 1915; Hemphill to Lingle, December 6, 1915; Boyd and Brackenridge, "The Evolving Role of the Southern Presbyterian Woman," 212; and undated sermons in Lingle Papers, "The Family and Social Problems" and "Poverty and Social Problems."
88. Dunbar H. Ogden to W. L. Lingle, January 2, 1913, January 15, 1914, March 30, 1915, October 14, 1915, October 30, 1913; all in Lingle Papers.
89. Theron H. Rice to W. L. Lingle, April 15, 1902; Rev. C. I. Stacy to W. L. Lingle, November 16, 1908; Stacy to Lingle, November 10, 1908; R. P. Smith to W. L. Lingle, April 22, 1909; John Eagan to W. L. Lingle, April 26, 1909; Eagan to Lingle, September 23, 1911; Lingle to Eagan, January 31, 1912; Eagan to Lingle, April 10, 1913; Eagan to Lingle, December 17, 1910; all in Lingle Papers.

90. John J. Eagan to W. L. Lingle, August 10, 1912, Lingle Papers.
91. Harry G. Lefever, "The Involvement of the Men and Religion Forward Movement in the Cause of Labor Justice, Atlanta, Georgia, 1912–1916," *Labor History*,(Fall 1973), 521–535; John J. Eagan to W. L. Lingle, April 4, 1916, Lingle Papers.
92. For an excellent though obviously subjective summary of Eagan's career, see Robert E. Speer, *John J. Eagan: A Memoir of an Adventurer For the Kingdom of God on Earth* (Birmingham: American Cast Iron Pipe Company, 1939).
93. Witherspoon Dodge to W. L. Lingle, December 15, 1913, October 27, 1916, February 28, 1917; Lingle Papers.
94. *Presbyterian Standard*, September 18, 1912.
95. *Ibid.*, September 4, 1918; R. C. Reed to W. L. Lingle, March 21, 1913, September 15, 1916; Lingle to Reed, September 12, 1916; Lingle Papers.
96. *Presbyterian Standard*, August 28, December 4, 1918, June 11, August 20 and 27, November 12, 1919.
97. Marcholl, *The Presbyterian Church in Alabama*, 340.
98. For an excellent discussion of the PCUS and the Federal Council of Churches, see Thompson, *Presbyterians in the South, Vol. III. 1900–1972*, 248–301.
99. *Presbyterian Standard*, May 29, 1912; *Minutes of the PCUS, 1913*, 67; *ibid.*, *1914*, 48; *ibid.*, *1915*, 39–40; *ibid.*, *1919*, 55.
100. Charles S. MacFarland to W. L. Lingle, March 26 and September 15, 1913; A. M. Scales to W. L. Lingle, March 20, 1913; Lingle Papers; *Presbyterian Standard*, April 3, 1912.
101. T. A. Painter to W. L. Lingle, March 29, 1920, Lingle Papers; *Presbyterian Standard*, March 17 and May 19, 1920.
102. W. L. Lingle to Rev. Jere A. Moore, April 4, 1911, Lingle Papers; *Presbyterian Standard*, February 6 and April 24, 1918.
103. For progress of the debate, see the *Presbyterian Standard*, February 26, March 12 and 26, August 13 and 20, September 24, October 15 and 29, November 12, December 3, 17, 19, 1919; W. L. Lingle to Rev. A. M. Fraser, September 8, 1919, Lingle Papers; *Minutes of the PCUS, 1919*, 47–48.
104. W. M. McPheeters to W. L. Lingle, May 19, 1920, Lingle Papers; *Presbyterian Standard*, November 12, 1919.
105. *Presbyterian Standard*, May 26, 1920; *Minutes of the PCUS, 1920*, 11; W. L. Lingle to Miss Mamie Bays, June 1, 1920; John Eagan to W. L. Lingle, June 4, 1920; W. L. Lingle to J. S. Lyons, June 1, 1920; Lingle Papers.
106. See Lingle's sermon, "The Bible and Poverty," and his discussion topics, "Christianity and the Depression," "Christianity and War," "The Church and Social Security"; Witherspoon Dodge, "Free Enterprise," unpublished manuscript in Stetson Kennedy Papers, Southern Labor Archives, Georgia State University, Atlanta, Georgia.

Notes to RELIGION AND POLITICS
by Samuel S. Hill

1. For a summary of the strength and profile of the "Electronic Church" ministry, see William F. Fore, "Religion and Television: Report on the Research," *Christian Century*, July 18–25, 1984, 710–713.

2. Michael L. Mezey, "The Minds of the South," in *Religion and Politics in the South*, eds. Tod A. Baker, Robert P. Steed, Laurence W. Moreland (New York: Praeger, 1983), 22.

3. Michael Lienesch, "Right-Wing Religion: Christian Conservatism as a Political Movement," *Political Science Quarterly* 97 (Fall 1982), 409.

4. James L. Guth, "Preachers and Politics: Varieties of Activism among Southern Baptist Ministers," in *Religion and Politics in the South*, 177, 181.

5. Lienesch, "Right-Wing Religion," 408, 407.

6. See John Patrick McDowell, *The Social Gospel in the South: The Woman's Home Mission Movement in the Methodist Episcopal Church, South, 1886–1939* (Baton Rouge: Louisiana State University Press, 1982).

7. J. Wayne Flynt has done a great deal, and more than anyone else, to bring instances of southern Social Gospel concerns to light.

8. See Donald G. Mathews, *Religion in the Old South* (Chicago: University of Chicago Press, 1977).

9. See Robert F. Martin, "Critique of Southern Society and Vision of a New Order: The Fellowship of Southern Churchmen, 1934–1957," *Church History* 52 (March 1983), 66–80.

10. Richard Nutt, "The Jesus That Stirred Up the People: Christian Faith in Action in the Southern Tenant Farmers' Union," paper presented at Conference on Religion and Political Activism, University of Southern Mississippi, April 4, 1984.

11. This is a theme found throughout Donald G. Mathews's published work.

12. See Rhys Isaac, *The Transformation of Virginia, 1740–1790* (Chapel Hill: University of North Carolina Press, 1982).

13. Jerry Perkins, Donald Fairchild, and Murray Havens, "The Effects of Evangelicalism on Southern Black and White Political Attitudes and Political Behavior," in Baker, Steed, and Moreland, *Religion and Politics*, 79.

14. Michael L. Mezey, "Minds of the South," 22.

15. *Ibid.*, 21.

16. *Ibid.*, 22.

17. Corwin Smidt, "Born-Again Politics: The Political Behavior of Evangelical Christians in the South and non-South," in *Religion and Politics*, 45.

18. Perkins, Fairchild, and Havens, "Effects of Evangelicalism," 80.

19. Kenneth D. Wald and Michael B. Lupfer, "Religion and Political Attitudes in the Urban South" in Baker, Steed, and Moreland, *Religion and Politics*, 94.

20. Baker, Steed, and Moreland, "Fundamentalist Belief and Southern Distinctiveness," in Baker, Steed, and Moreland, *Religion and Politics*, 140.

21. See James J. Thompson, *Tried As By Fire: Southern Baptists in the 1920s* (Macon, Ga.: Mercer University Press, 1982).

22. Smidt, "Born-Again Politics," 51.

23. Baker, Steed, and Moreland, *Religion and Politics*, 140.

24. Smidt, "Born-Again Politics," 51.

25. Michael L. Mezey, "Minds of the South," 22.

Notes to REGIONALISM IN AMERICAN RELIGION
by Edwin S. Gaustad

1. In 1972 and again in 1977, National Pastoral Hispanic Conferences (Encuentros) were held to deal with the long-neglected concerns of the Hispanic Catholic

minority. Then in 1983, a Pastoral Letter on the *Hispanic Presence* emanated from the nation's Roman Catholic bishops; it was published by the U.S. Catholic Conference in 1984.

2. See, for example, C. Eric Lincoln, ed., *The Black Experience in Religion* (Garden City, N.Y.: Anchor Books, 1974); Milton Sernett, *Black Religion and American Evangelicalism* (Metuchen, N.J.: Scarecrow Press, 1975); Albert J. Raboteau, *Slave Religion* (New York: Oxford University Press, 1978); and James H. Cone's and G. S. Wilmore's exceptionally valuable anthology, *Black Theology* (New York: Orbis, 1979).

3. Books dealing with the religious dimensions of feminism have multiplied rapidly, among them these solid studies: Rosemary Ruether and Eleanor McLaughlin, *Women of Spirit* (New York: Simon and Schuster, 1979); Leonard and Arlene Swidler, *Women Priests* (New York: Paulist Press, 1977); and Phyllis Trible, *God and the Rhetoric of Sexuality* (Philadelphia: Fortress Press, 1978).

4. John B. Boles, "Religion in the South: A Tradition Recovered," *Maryland Historical Magazine*, 77 (Winter 1980).

5. Edwin S. Gaustad, *Historical Atlas of Religion in America* (Rev. ed.; New York: Harper and Row, 1976), Fig. 12.

6. *Ibid.*, Fig. 14.

7. *Ibid.*, Fig. 8.

8. *Ibid.*, Fig. 64.

9. *Ibid.*, Fig. 56.

10. *Ibid.*, Fig. 89.

11. See Francis J. Weber, ed., *Documents of Catholic California History* (Los Angeles: Dawson's Book Shop, 1965), 102f.

12. *Historical Atlas*, Fig. 105.

13. *Ibid.*, color fold-out map in jacket.

14. Eugene Boe, as found in Thomas C. Wheeler, ed., *The Immigrant Experience* (New York: Dial Press, 1971).

15. *Historical Atlas*, Fig. 50.

16. *Ibid.*, Fig. 82.

17. *Ibid.*, Fig. 83.

18. *Ibid.*, Fig. 101.

19. *Ibid.*, Fig. 113.

20. *Ibid.*, color fold-out map in jacket.

21. For all the data in this section, see Bernard Quinn et al., *Churches and Church Membership in the United States: 1980* (Atlanta, Ga.: Glenmary Research Center, 1982). For some religious comparisons of the South with the East, West, and Midwest, see the latest Gallup Report (#222), *Religion in America* (1984).

22. Many recent books address this large question, not all of them of course from identical stances. See, for example, Philip Slater, *The Pursuit of Loneliness* (rev. ed.; Boston: Beacon Press, 1976); Christopher Lasch, *The Culture of Narcissism* (New York: Norton, 1978); Robert N. Bellah, *The Broken Covenant* (New York: Seabury Press, 1975); Mary Douglas and Steven M. Tipton, eds., *Religion and America: Spirituality in a Secular Age* (Boston: Beacon Press, 1983); and Richard John Neuhaus, *The Naked Public Square* (Grand Rapids, Mich.: Eerdman's, 1984).

Selected Bibliography

The purpose of this selected bibliography is to provide the reader with a general guide to the literature on southern religious development. It is not designed nor intended to be a complete listing. Readers should check the notes to each essay for exact sources used by each individual author.

Baer, Hans A. *The Black Spiritual Movement: A Religious Re sponse to Racism.* Knoxville: University of Tennessee Press, 1984.

Baker, Tod A., Robert P. Steed, and Laurence W. Moreland, eds. *Religion and Politics in the South: Mass and Elite Perspectives.* New York: Praeger Publishers, 1983.

Bailey, Kenneth K. "Protestantism and Afro-Americans in the Old South: Another Look." *Journal of Southern History* 41 (November 1975), 451–472.

———. *Southern White Protestantism in the Twentieth Century.* New York: Harper & Row, 1964.

Bode, Frederick A. *Protestantism and the New South: North Carolina Baptists and Methodists in Political Crisis, 1894– 1903.* Charlottesville: University of Virginia Press, 1975.

Boles, John B. *The Great Revival 1787–1805: The Origins of the Southern Evangelical Mind.* Lexington: University Press of Kentucky, 1972.

———. *Religion in Antebellum Kentucky.* Lexington: University Press of Kentucky, 1976.

———. "Religion in the South: A Tradition Recovered." *Maryland Historical Magazine* 77 (December 1982), 388–401.

Bolton, C. Charles. *Southern Anglicanism: The Church of England in Colonial South Carolina.* Westport Conn.: Greenwood Press, 1982.

Bruce, Dickson D., Jr. *And They All Sang Hallelujah: Plain-Folk Camp-Meeting Religion, 1800–1845.* Knoxville: University of Tennessee Press, 1974.

————. "Religion, Society and Culture in the Old South: A Comparative View." *American Quarterly* 26 (October 1974), 399–416.

Cobb, Buell E., Jr. *The Sacred Harp: A Tradition and Its Music.* Athens: University of Georgia Press, 1978.

Cone, James. *For My People: Black Theology and the Black Church.* Maryknoll, New York: Orbis, 1984.

Connelly, Thomas L. *Will Campbell and the Soul of the South.* New York: Continuum, 1982.

Daniel, W. Harrison. "The Effects of the Civil War on Southern Protestantism." *Maryland Historical Magazine* 69 (Spring 1974), 44–63.

Dinnerstein, Leonard, and Mary Dale Palsson, eds. *Jews in the South.* Baton Rouge: Louisiana State University Press, 1973.

Earle, John R., Dean D. Knudsen, and Donald W. Shriver. *Spindles and Spires: A Re-Study of Religion and Social Change in Gastonia.* Atlanta: John Knox Press, 1976.

Eighmy, John Lee. *Churches in Cultural Captivity: A History of the Social Attitudes of Southern Baptists.* Knoxville: University of Tennessee Press, 1972.

Evans, Eli. *The Provincials: A Personal History of Jews in the South.* New York: Atheneum, 1976.

Farish, Hunter D. *The Circuit-Rider Dismounts: A Social History of Southern Methodism, 1865–1900.* Richmond: Dietz Press, 1938.

Friedman, Jean E. *The Enclosed Garden: Women in the Evangelical South, 1825–1885* (forthcoming).

Harrell, David E., Jr. *All Things Are Possible: The Healing and Charismatic Revivals in Modern America.* Bloomington: Indiana University Press, 1975.

————. *Quest For a Christian America: The Disciples of Christ and American Society to 1866.* Nashville: Disciples of Christ Historical Society, 1966.

————. "The Sectional Origins of the Churches of Christ." *Journal of Southern History* 30 (August 1964), 261–77.

————. ed. *Varieties of Southern Evangelicalism.* Macon, Ga: Mercer University Press, 1981.

————. *White Sects and Black Men in the Recent South.* Nashville: Vanderbilt University Press, 1971.

Hill, Samuel S., Jr., ed. *Encyclopedia of Southern Religion.* Macon, Ga: Mercer University Press, 1983.

————. ed. *On Jordan's Stormy Banks.* Macon, Ga.: Mercer University Press, 1983.

————. et al. *Religion and the Solid South.* Nashville: Abingdon Press, 1972.

————. ed. *Religion in the Southern States,* Macon, Ga: Mercer University Press, 1983.

————. *The South and the North in American Religion.* Athens: University of Georgia Press, 1980.

————. *Southern Churches in Crisis.* New York, Chicago, and San Francisco: Holt, Rinehart and Winston, 1966.

Holifield, E. Brooks. *Gentlemen Theologians: American Theology in Southern Culture, 1795–1860.* Durham, N.C.: Duke University Press, 1978.

Isaac, Rhys. *The Transformation of Virginia, 1780–1790.* Chapel Hill, N.C.: Published for the Institute of Early American History and Culture by the University of North Carolina Press, 1982.

Kane, Steven M. "Holy Ghost People: The Snake-Handlers of Southern Appalachia." *Appalachian Journal* 1 (Summer 1974), 255–262.

Kurtz, Ernest. "The Tragedy of Southern Religion." *Georgia Historical Quarterly* 66 (Summer 1982), 217–247.

Lincoln, C. Eric, ed. *The Black Experience in Religion.* Garden City, New York: Anchor Press/Doubleday, 1974.

————. *Race, Religion, and The Continuing American Dilemma.* New York: Hill & Wang, 1984.

Lippy, Charles H., ed. *Bibliography of Religion in the South.* Macon, Ga: Mercer University Press, 1985.

Loveland, Anne C., *Southern Evangelicals and the Social Order, 1800–1860.* Baton Rouge: Louisiana State University Press, 1980.

Martin, Robert F. "Critique of Southern Society and Vision of a New Order: The Fellowship of Southern Churchmen, 1934–1957." *Church History* 52 (March 1983), 66–80.

Mathews, Donald G., *Religion in the Old South*. Chicago: University of Chicago Press, 1977.

————. *Slavery and Methodism: A Chapter in American Morality, 1780–1845*. Princeton: Princeton University Press, 1965.

Miller, Randall M., and Jon L. Wakelyn, eds. *Catholics in the Old South: Essays on Church and Culture*. Macon, Ga.: Mercer University Press, 1984.

Peterson, Thomas V. *Ham and Japheth: The Mythic World of Whites in the Antebellum South*. Metuchen, N.J., and London: Scarecrow Press, 1978.

Pope, Liston. *Millhands and Preachers: A Study of Gastonia*. New Haven: Yale University Press, 1942.

Proctor, Samuel, and Louis Schmier, with Malcolm Stern, eds. *Jews of the South: Selected Essays*. Macon, Ga.: Mercer University Press, 1984.

Raboteau, Albert J. *Slave Religion: The "Invisible Institution" in the Antebellum South*. New York: Oxford University Press, 1978.

Reed, John Shelton. *The Enduring South: Sub-Cultural Persistence in a Mass Society*. Chapel Hill: University of North Carolina Press, 1972.

Scott, Anne Firor. *The Southern Lady: From Pedestal to Politics, 1830–1930*. Chicago: University of Chicago Press, 1970.

Shortridge, James R. "A New Regionalization of American Religion." *Journal for the Scientific Study of Religion* 16 (June 1977), 143–153.

Smith, H. Shelton. *In His Image, But . . . Racism in Southern Religion, 1780–1910*. Durham, N.C.: Duke University Press, 1972.

Spain, Rufus B. *At Ease in Zion: A Social History of Southern Baptists, 1865–1900*. Nashville: Vanderbilt University Press, 1967.

Sutton, Brett. "Primitive Baptist Vision Narratives." *Perspectives on the American South*. New York, London & Paris: Gordon & Breach, 1981, Volume I.

Synan, Vinson. *The Holiness-Pentecostal Movement in the United States*. Grand Rapids, Michigan: William B. Eerdmans Publishing Company, 1971.

Thompson, Ernest Trice. *Presbyterians in the South.* 3 volumes, Richmond: John Knox Press, 1963–73.

Thompson, James J., Jr. *"Tried as by Fire.": Southern Baptists and the Religious Controversies of the 1920s.* Macon, Ga.: Mercer University Press, 1982.

Walker, Clarence E. *A Rock in a Weary Land: The African Methodist Episcopal Church During the Civil War and Reconstruction.* Baton Rouge: Louisiana State University Press, 1982.

Washington, Joseph R., Jr. *Black Religion: The Negro and Christianity in the United States.* Boston: Beacon Press, 1964.

Wight, Willard E. "The Churches and the Confederate Cause." *Civil War History* 6 (December 1960), 361–73.

Wilson, Charles Reagan. *Baptized in Blood: The Religion of the Lost Cause, 1865–1920.* Athens: University of Georgia Press, 1980.

Yance, Norman A. *Religion Southern Style: Southern Baptists and Society in Historical Perspective.* Macon, Ga.: Mercer University Press, 1978.

Contributors

John B. Boles is Professor of History at Rice University and editor of the *Journal of Southern History*. His works include *Black Southerners, 1619–1869* and *The Great Revival: Origins of the Southern Evangelical Mind, 1787–1805*.

C. Eric Lincoln is Professor of Religion and Culture at Duke University. He is the author of many books including *Race, Religion, and the Continuing American Dilemma* and *The Black Muslims in America*.

David Edwin Harrell, Jr. is Distinguished Professor of History at the University of Arkansas. His many works include *Quest for a Christian America: The Disciples of Christ and American Society to 1866* and *All Things are Possible: The Healing and Charismatic Revivals in Modern America*.

J. Wayne Flynt is Professor of History at Auburn University. He is the author of *Dixie's Forgotten People: The South's Poor Whites, Cracker Messiah: Governor Sidney J. Catts of Florida*, and other books.

Samuel S. Hill, Jr. is Professor of Religion at the University of Florida. His publications include *Southern Churches in Crisis* and an edited reference book, the *Encyclopedia of Religion in the South*.

Edwin Scott Gaustad is Professor of History at the University of California at Riverside. He is the author of the *Historical Atlas of Religion in America, A Religious History of America*, and other works.

Index

Abortion, and New Christian Right, 140–41
African Methodist Episcopal Church, 50
African Methodist Episcopal Church, Zion, 49, 50, 170
African ritual, 53
Ahlstrom, Sydney E., 11
Alabama Baptist Association, 56
Alexander, Will, 87
Allen, Richard, 50
American Baptist Association, 71, 170
American Cast Iron Pipe Company, 130, 137
American Inland Mission, 94
Amish, 147
Anabaptists, 147
Anderson, Ramele, 114
Anglican Church, 11. See also Church of England; Episcopal Church.
Anti-Catholicism, 8, 61
Anti-Semitism, 61
Antimission movement, 66
Appalachia, PCUS mission work in, 96–98
Arminianism, 63
Articles of Confederation, 18
Asbury, Francis, 28–29, 55
Asheville Presbytery, 94
Assembly of God, 78, 170
Associated Reformed Presbyterian Church, 113
Association of Southern Women for the Prevention of Lynching, 142
Atlanta Constitution, 130
Attleboro (PA), 49
Austin Seminary, 123
Averyt, Agnes, 114
Azusa Street meeting, 77

Baer, Hans A., 6
Bailey, Kenneth K., 4, 7, 13
Baker, Ray Stannard, 83
Bakker, Jim, 3, 139–40
Balfour, Arthur J., 110
Baptist Church, as "culture religion," 11, 163–64; as sect, 8; becomes middle-class, 69–70; discipline in, 17; effect of Great Revival on, 24; F. E. Wallace on dominance of, 61; in colonial America, 159; mis-

sionary work among blacks, 41–42; revival of in Virginia, 16; similarity to Churches of Christ, 63; mentioned, 11
Baptist Church of Christ, 63
Baptist Missionary Association, 170
The Baptist and Commoner, 71
Barbecue, 46
Bascom, Henry, 65
Beene and Arkansas Camp Meeting Association, 81
Benedict, David, 67
Bently, George, 56
Berkeley, Dean, 38
Bethel African Methodist Episcopal Church, 49
Bethel Methodist Church, 49
"Betty," 48
Beyer, Alida, 99
Birmingham (AL), 74–75, 106
"Black Harry," (Harry Hosier), 55
Black churches, 47–52
Black ministers, ordained in Methodist Church, 50
Black religion, 35–57
Blacks, and New Christian Right, 141–42; and politico-religious beliefs, 147; development of separate religions among, 6–7; Walter L. Lingle on, 111; welcomed in antebellum Baptist and Methodist churches, 28
Blassingame, John W., 7
Blue Ridge Academy, 95
Bode, Frederick, 79
Bogard, Ben M., 71
Boles, John B., 5–7, 60, 156
Bradstreet, Simon, 38
Brown, Raymond, 80
Brush arbors, 39
Bryan, Andrew, 54

Caddo Valley School, 95
"Caesar," 56
Calvin, John, 108, 147
Calvinism, 63, 67, 148
Camp meeting, attitude of Methodists, Bap-

195